Presented To:

_____

From:

_____

Date:

_____

# WISDOM for WINNERS

## VOLUME FOUR

# WISDOM *for* WINNERS

## VOLUME FOUR

# JIM STOVALL

AN OFFICIAL PUBLICATION OF
**THE NAPOLEON HILL FOUNDATION**

SOUND WISDOM

P.O. Box 310

Shippensburg, PA 17257-0310

International rights inquiries please contact The Napoleon Hill Foundation at 276-328-6700

Email: napoleonhill@uvawise.edu

For more information on foreign distributors, call 717-532-3040.

Or reach us on the Internet: www.soundwisdom.com

ISBN 13 HC: 978-1-64095-000-9

ISBN 13 EBook: 978-1-64095-001-6

For Worldwide Distribution, Printed in the U.S.A.

1 2 3 4 5 6 / 21 20 19 18

Cover/Jacket design by Eileen Rockwell

Interior design by Terry Clifton

# CONTENTS

# FOREWORD

PERHAPS YOU ARE ONE OF THE MILLIONS OF PEOPLE WHO have enjoyed the more than 30 books written by Jim Stovall over the years. You may have even watched one of the movies that were made from Jim Stovall's books. Jim's best-selling book, *The Ultimate Gift*, with more than five million copies sold, was one of the books made into a movie. *The Ultimate Gift* movie grossed over $110 million.

And perhaps you have read the first three editions of *Wisdom for Winners*. If so, you know the wit and wisdom that awaits you in this fourth volume—and you won't be disappointed. When Jim Stovall writes a column on wealth and life, he does so with authority.

Jim Stovall's *Wisdom for Winners* is a collection of columns that millions of people have read over the years. His wisdom and experience on a particular subject provide a great amount of credibility to his writings. Even though Jim has written several articles on overcoming adversity, perhaps for those who do not know his background, a little personal information is worth knowing. Jim aspired to be an NFL player and he had the mental and physical capabilities to be a success. Also, Jim was a heavy-weight Olympic weight lifter, but his plans took a serious challenge.

While attending Oral Roberts University, Jim was diagnosed with macular degeneration, which led to him becoming blind. Tutored by his girlfriend, Jim graduated. Most people going blind would just give up and seek government assistance. Not Jim. He told his dad (who was an employee of Oral Roberts University) that he wanted to work for himself. Jim's father introduced Jim to Lee Braxton, a large financial contributor to Oral Roberts University.

Jim was fortunate to be introduced to Braxton, as he was a great example of overcoming adversity and founder of many successful companies, including a bank. Lee Braxton was also a close friend of Napoleon Hill and delivered Hill's eulogy when he died in 1970. Braxton had used the principles found in Napoleon Hill's book *Think and Grow Rich,* and not only learned them, but took action. Braxton introduced Jim Stovall to *Think and Grow Rich,* which helped him become successful in financial and personal matters.

You will certainly be rewarded for reading Jim Stovall's columns on the value of wealth, learning is a life-long process, mastering your time, doing your best, looking for opportunities, what is important in life, and many other articles found in this volume of *Wisdom for Winners.*

While Jim's columns often provide financial advice, his columns also cover important topics such as "What is Important in Life." Jim gives advice on giving that creates a legacy for the giver. Jim tells us that while budgeting our money and making investments can benefit our family, it can also put us in a position to help others.

A favorite quote of mine from Stovall's *The Millionaire Map,* published by Sound Wisdom, simply states, "Never accept a map from someone who has not been where you want to go." If you would consider that simple statement and the good advice behind it, it could make the difference between you being successful, or just being one of the majority of people who are not.

Jim also wrote a book titled *The Financial Crossroads: The Intersection of Money and Life,* co-authored with Timothy J. Maurer, a certified financial planner. Jim reminds his readers that being motivated is useless if you do not know what to do. Knowing what to do is useless unless you are motivated to act.

Jim Stovall writes from his own personal experiences. For example, Jim has provided 500 scholarships for students attending Oral Roberts University. Jim has made many contributions, such as the articles you are about to read. Jim gave his many columns to the nonprofit Napoleon Hill Foundation to raise funds to provide scholarships for the University of Virginia's College at Wise. The Napoleon Hill Foundation also does prison work and has worked to make the success principles available around the world to make the world a better place in which to live.

I hope you enjoy the book, one column of wisdom at a time. Steve Forbes, publisher of *Forbes* magazine, calls Jim, "One of the most outstanding men of this era."

—DON M. GREEN, executive director of The Napoleon Hill Foundation, board member of the University of Virginia/Wise, and president of the University of Virginia/Wise Foundation.

# INTROSPECTION

# PLAY IT AGAIN

APPROXIMATELY ONE IN A THOUSAND BOOKS WRITTEN EVER gets published and makes it to the bestseller list, and approximately one in a thousand books on the bestseller list are ever made into a movie, which is about the same odds of having a successful book and a sequel; therefore, I was grateful and humble as this 33rd book was released. *Wisdom for Winners Volume 4* is a sequel to *Wisdom for Winners* released through my publisher Sound Wisdom in conjunction with The Napoleon Hill Foundation. (Visit www.JimStovallBooks.com.)

I also owe a great debt of gratitude to you. The popularity of my weekly columns for 20 years is sustained because of the readers, and these new books are made up of a compilation of my weekly columns put together by Don Green who runs The Napoleon Hill Foundation and also wrote the Foreword to all four volumes.

All of the profits from each volume of *Wisdom for Winners* is being donated to The Napoleon Hill Foundation. I am very pleased and excited to be able to support their work because the work of Napoleon Hill which began a century ago has contributed mightily to my success and the success of untold people around the world.

Napoleon Hill was best known for his landmark book titled *Think and Grow Rich*. Dr. Hill was among the first to declare that wealth was not a product of luck or being born into the right family, but instead, wealth was the natural result of thinking and acting in certain prescribed and logical ways.

Napoleon Hill didn't merely guess or speculate how someone could be successful and create wealth. Instead, he approached Andrew Carnegie, one of the wealthiest men of the day, and asked him the key to success. Carnegie encouraged Hill to discover the keys himself and share them with the world. Carnegie opened the door for Hill by introducing him to Thomas Edison, Henry Ford, Alexander Graham Bell, and hundreds of the most successful people of the day. The result of two decades of compiling and condensing this wisdom was Napoleon Hill's masterpiece *Think and Grow Rich*. That book paved the way for virtually all success and personal development writers, including me, for decades to come.

If you took all the money in the world and divided it up equally among everyone, within a few short years, the people who are enjoying wealth today would be wealthy again; and those who are now living in poverty would be poor again. Knowledge is the key to wealth. Not money.

As you go through your day today, seek wisdom instead of money, and you will have both.

Today's the day!

# CHANGE YOUR MIND
# AND YOUR LIFE

B EHAVIORAL SCIENTISTS HAVE LONG DEBATED WHETHER WE are most impacted by nature or nurture. The argument is made up of professionals who believe we are products of our genetic makeup and those who believe we are molded by our environment. As a student of behavioral science, it's impossible for me to imagine we are not impacted both by our DNA as well as the world around us.

The element that most scientists overlook is that we all have the ability to change our minds. We can be born with certain abilities or disabilities but decide to pursue a myriad of possibilities within our lives. As a blind person myself due to a genetic disorder, I am limited in how I do certain things far more than which things I choose to do. I have written more than 30 books, and eight of them have been made into movies or are in production now. This means I write books I can't see that are made into movies I can't watch.

Recently, there have been extensive studies of twins who grew up in homes with alcoholic parents. These studies revealed that, given the same genetic makeup and environment, one sibling might become an incurable alcoholic while the other twin might choose to never touch a drop of alcohol throughout their life. We are impacted by our genetics and environment, but we get to choose how we are impacted.

My late, great colleague and mentor Dr. Wayne Dyer bought a house on the beach in a new development in Hawaii. Every day as Dr. Dyer walked on the beach, he encountered new neighbors who were moving into the development. One morning he confronted a gentleman who had just moved to Hawaii from New Jersey. The gentleman asked Dr. Dyer, "What are people like here? Are they friendly?" Dr. Dyer considered it a moment and then asked, "What are people like where you come from?" The gentleman blurted out, "They are rude, thoughtless, and annoying." Dr. Dyer responded, "You'll find people to be about the same here."

As Dr. Dyer continued his walk, he was confronted by an elderly lady who had just relocated from Nebraska. She asked, "Are the residents here nice?" Dr. Dyer inquired, "Are people nice where you come from?" She smiled and said, enthusiastically, "Yes! People in Nebraska are friendly, giving, and loving." Dr. Dyer smiled and stated, "You'll find people here in Hawaii to be just the same."

Environment and heredity determine where we start, but we determine where we finish.

As you go through your day today, embrace the good, reject the bad, and create the life you want.

*Today's the day!*

# BE A FANATIC

RECENTLY, I HEARD SEVERAL COLLEAGUES ENGAGING IN A conversation about a competitor in our industry. They described this individual as a "fanatic." He was, in turn, said to be "over-the-top," "out-of-control," and "absolutely outrageous." I thought about these descriptions and realized that in the proper context, these are success traits that I admire. I am not, in this case, referring to those misguided souls and evil people whose fanaticism damages or destroys others; but instead, in this context, fanaticism refers to a passion and enthusiasm shared by top performers.

I have written a book titled *Ultimate Hindsight* (www.JimStovallBooks.com) In this book, I share advice that I have received from more than 100 top performers in the fields of business, sports, politics, and entertainment regarding things they know now that they wish they had known when they began.

To someone on the outside looking in, each of these peak performers could be described as a fanatic. I think we all should be fanatical about the right things at the right time. I hope you're fanatical about your spouse, your children, your career, and your country.

I am a huge fan of sports. The term is actually a derivative of fanatic. At any given time at football stadiums, basketball arenas, or baseball diamonds, you will see otherwise reserved and orderly people jumping up and down, screaming wildly, wearing outrageous costumes, painting their faces, or other fanatical behavior. We do not generally find it to be strange that those people are fanatical in those times and places.

All of us should be surrounded by people and engaged in pursuits that bring us unbridled energy, outrageous optimism, and simple joy. Life is too short to live any other way. It's not a question of should we be fanatical or not. It's a matter of all of us becoming fanatical about the right things.

I remember having the privilege of meeting champion golfer Lee Trevino. He described the grueling grind of the professional golf tour involving an unbelievable schedule of travel, publicity commitments, and high-pressure golf tournaments week after week. He went on to explain that each year, at the end of the season, he would stagger home, throw his golf clubs in the garage, and declare, "I'm never playing golf again!" Mr. Trevino then said he generally slept for 18 hours, spent some quality time with his wife and family, and then rushed out into the garage, threw his golf clubs into the trunk of his car, and raced toward the nearest golf course. Golf is Lee Trevino's vocation and avocation. It is his job, his hobby, and his passion.

The greatest wish I could have for you is that you find something to do with your life that turns you into a fanatic.

As you go through your day today, don't eliminate or dilute your fanaticism. Just refocus it.

*Today's the day!*

# LUNCH AT THE WHITE HOUSE

ALL OF US HAVE MILESTONES AND MEMORIES ALONG LIFE'S journey that can serve to remind us where we've been, where we are, and where we are going. I had the privilege of accepting an invitation to have lunch at the White House. I chose to look upon it as more of a patriotic than a political experience. As I walked through the gates and entered into the West Wing of the White House, I realized that the moment would be indelibly printed in my mental scrapbook of my own success journey.

Over a quarter of a century ago, I woke up one morning and instantly realized that I had lost the remainder of my sight, and I knew I would live the rest of my life as a blind person. The thoughts, doubts, and fears that came over me that morning would be impossible to describe to you. I was 29 years old, had never met a blind person, and I didn't have a clue what I was going to do with the rest of my life.

The only plan I could come up with that fateful morning involved moving into a little 9- by 12-foot room in the back of my house where I literally thought I would live out the rest of my life. The thought of traveling millions of miles and speaking to millions of people in arena events, running a television network with more than 1,000 stations, writing over 30 books and having six of them turned into major motion pictures, or writing weekly columns read by countless people around the world seemed as foreign to me as going to the moon. I simply could not imagine it as I sat in my 9- by 12-foot self-imposed prison.

Each day, we all get to decide who we are and what we are going to do. I am still that person trapped in a 9- by 12-foot room just as much as I am the person who has received an Emmy Award, a gold medal, the International Humanitarian honor, and had lunch at the White House.

Our memories can take us back to the very best or the very worst places in our past. We can revisit all of the thoughts and emotions that brought us either success or failure. We choose daily which page in the scrapbook to revisit. If you choose the mountain-top moments to replay in your mind, you will find yourself moving from victory to victory. If you wallow in the memories of your defeats, you are destined to relive them. Charles Dickens may have said it best when he wrote, "It was the best of times, it was the worst of times."

As you go through your day today, remember the mountain-top or the White House.

*Today's the day!*

# ELEVATE YOUR MIND

I HATE TO BE THE ONE TO GIVE YOU THE BAD NEWS, BUT LIFE IS not fair. Life is great, it's grand, and it's wonderful, as well as being the only game in town—but it's not fair. We don't always get what we want, need, or even deserve, but we will always eventually get what we expect.

Our vision drives our expectations, which drives our performance, which creates our results. You cannot outperform the vision you have of yourself. You may think it odd to be getting advice from a blind person about vision; however, vision is the opposite in many ways of sight. Sight tells you where you are and what's around you. Vision tells you where you could be and what is possible.

My mentor and friend Jack Nicklaus often says, "I never hit a successful golf shot until I visualize it in my mind going exactly where I want it to go."

In order to supercharge our vision, we often need to get away from the mundane and ordinary elements of life to explore the realm of possibility. Pablo Picasso said, "Art washes away from the soul the dust of everyday life." Oftentimes, we get so caught up in maintaining the status quo that we forget to consider the universe of options and opportunities. It's easy to become so busy making a living that we forget to make a life.

There are certain works of literature and pieces of music that can elevate my thinking and get me away from the day-to-day routine of responsibilities. It's important, periodically, to rise above the fray, gain a new perspective, and evaluate your course. Habits are good and can serve us well within our daily routine, but we must form an additional habit of re-examining the routine so that we can be not only productive but creative.

My friend and colleague Paula Marshall and I wrote a book together entitled *The Executive Entrepreneur*. Paula is the third-generation CEO of a multimillion dollar, multinational company, and I am a startup entrepreneur. Paula and I discovered that executives need elements of entrepreneurship to stay current and creative, and entrepreneurs need executive training to manage what they have built.

As you go through your day today, take care of the here and now, but consider the realm of possibilities.

*Today's the day!*

# FIRST WORLD AND THIRD WORLD PROBLEMS

I'VE BEEN WRITING MY WEEKLY COLUMNS FOR 20 YEARS. WHEN I first began writing *Winners' Wisdom*, it only appeared in the local business journal in my hometown. Then it began to grow as more newspapers and magazines picked up my weekly effort. The popularity of the column seemed to reach critical mass at about the same time online publications became available around the world. Today via newspapers, magazines, and online publications, my weekly efforts are read in virtually every part of the world by people from diverse backgrounds, faiths, and socioeconomic groups.

Many readers take advantage of the contact information and email me. I have had ongoing correspondence with a number of readers for many years. Some of them live in the United States as I do, but many others live in remote parts of the globe that I had not previously known of. Extensive travel and contact with all types of people offer a new perspective.

Here in America, it is easy to confuse problems with inconveniences. When your cell phone drops a call, your car battery dies, or a telemarketer phones you while you're eating dinner, this is not a crisis nor is it even a problem. It is an inconvenience.

Here in America, we struggle against obesity in a world that is malnourished. We run promotional ads for people to drink water and remain hydrated when a major cause of death and disease worldwide is lack of clean drinking water. We complain about traffic when, worldwide, many people do not know the benefits or even the convenience of being able to travel where they want to go at any time. If you and I can keep a worldwide perspective and be mindful of third world problems, we can eliminate much of the annoyance we feel with first world inconveniences.

I have met a number of people who have relocated to the United States from third world countries. Many of them are entrepreneurs who attend my speaking events. Their success within our free enterprise system can put many native-born Americans to shame when you realize these transplanted entrepreneurs deal with many language and cultural barriers unknown to the rest of us.

Our country is far from perfect, and there are many challenges we need to face and resolve, but may we never forget that the whole world would love to trade their problems for our inconveniences and live the dream life that we, too often, take for granted.

As you go through your day today, try to overlook inconveniences and help others who have real problems.

*Today's the day!*

# THE GRATITUDE GIFT

I N OUR COMMERCIALIZED, MEDIA-DRIVEN SOCIETY, THE holiday season has become something urgent instead of something important. My late, great friend and mentor Dr. Stephen Covey taught us all in his book *The 7 Habits of Highly Effective People* that *important* things are activities that are vital to us, our loved ones, and the things we care about. *Urgent* things are activities that are thrust at us or upon us by outside forces and have nothing to do with what really matters to us.

The holiday season begins earlier every year if you follow the commercial ads and media hype. I fear it won't be long until the blessed holidays of our ancestors will become year-'round sales and marketing opportunities. Thanksgiving should be focused on family, fun, food, festivities, and faith. It is not necessarily a time to get more, have more, and consume more; but instead, it is a time to be thankful for what we already have been given.

Several years ago I wrote a book titled *The Ultimate Gift* and the movie based on that novel. I have written more than 30 books, and eight of them have been turned into movies with two more in production. But with all of those messages and stories, *The Ultimate Gift* stands out, and within that little novel, one simple message has probably resonated with more people than any other. That is, simply, *The Gift of Gratitude.* Gratitude is rarely thought of as a gift we receive but it may be among the most important and beneficial ideals we can embrace.

Within The Gift of Gratitude chapter in *The Ultimate Gift*, I share a concept that has proved to be powerful and enduring for countless people around the world. I simply call this concept *The Golden List*. I was introduced to The Golden List by my grandmother when I was very young. Apparently, my parents were dealing with a family crisis involving hospitalization, and I was spending several days with my grandparents in another state. As the story has been related to me over the years, I was very unhappy and upset about being away from my parents, my friends, and my toys, so I guess I was complaining a lot.

My grandmother changed my life and, in turn, the lives of untold numbers of people around the world when she said, "You can complain all you want just as soon as we fill out your Golden List." She took out a blank sheet of paper, titled it the Golden List, and encouraged me to name ten things I was thankful for as she wrote them down. This seemingly insignificant exercise is revolutionary.

I found it impossible then—as I do today a half-century later—to list ten things for which I was thankful and then complain about anything. The very process of calling to mind and putting onto paper what we are thankful for makes our complaints, concerns, and cares of the day simply fade into insignificance.

As you go through your day today, give yourself and those you love the *Gift of Gratitude* and *The Golden List*.

*Today's the day!*

# THE POWER OF DECONSTRUCTION

IF YOU LIVE IN AN URBAN OR METROPOLITAN AREA, YOU HAVE likely observed the process of a building being torn down to make room for a new building to be located in the same spot. Often, valuable pieces of property are covered by rundown or decaying buildings that are keeping the underlying value from being available and apparent.

This is true in our own lives as we often get into certain habits and patterns that become permanent fixtures without us making conscious decisions or even being aware that it is happening. Some of the most important decisions in our lives are made randomly whether we realize it or not. It is likely that you live in an area, work in an organization, and have established friendships and other relationships based more upon happenstance than proactive decisions.

From time to time, I like to look at every area of my life and go through a process I call deconstruction. Deconstruction involves answering simple questions that unravel the complexities in our past that have brought us to where we are in the present moment. Deconstruction questions might include: Why do you live where you live? What brought you to that location, and why have you stayed there? Why do you work in the field and at the organization where you work? What were the contacts and connections that resulted in the career you have today?

I have met many people who answered an employment ad decades ago and accepted a job in a certain field that required them to move to a new area where they and their family have been for many years. Deconstruction will reveal the random nature of the decisions that have resulted in major outcomes in their personal and professional lives without them even being aware of it.

If you go through the process of deconstruction and then determine you like and value where you are, this is a great outcome, and the deconstruction process has served you well. It's much like going to the doctor for a checkup and determining everything is okay. On the other hand, the process of deconstruction might reveal that you would be happier or more productive in another job, in another industry, located in a different city, state, or even country. Life is dynamic with many options and opportunities, but if we're not careful, inertia can take over, and we find ourselves a long way down a road we had never intended to travel.

It has been said that an unexamined life is not worth living. You may initially find the process of deconstruction somewhat uncomfortable or disturbing as it challenges established elements of your life, but once you fully explore the process, you will emerge with a new sense of control and possibility that had not existed previously.

A person who does not make choices or a person who doesn't realize they have choices is no better off than someone who doesn't have any choices at all.

As you go through your day today, consider deconstruction as a way to clear space for future greatness.

*Today's the day!*

# Inspiration and Perspiration

A<small>S THE AUTHOR OF ALMOST 40 BOOKS, EIGHT OF WHICH HAVE</small> been turned into movies, I am often asked where I find the inspiration for the stories. While I would never discount the importance of ideas that occur to me or any other creative person, I would have to admit that the process of creating any artistic endeavor is simply hard work.

We've all heard the stories or legends about great writers, artists, poets, or other creative individuals who go to their proverbial mountaintops and come back with a masterpiece fully formed. Every great writer I have ever spoken with confirms that they spend a lot of time agonizing as they stare at a blank page. Ernest Hemingway stated sarcastically, "Writing is easy. All you do is open up a vein and bleed."

The creative process is difficult and takes a toll on the person attempting to birth something worthy of an audience. The great painter Jean Renaud painted every day, and when his arthritis became so advanced that he could not hold a brush, he tied paintbrushes to his hands. The legendary composer, Joseph Hayden, rose every day at dawn to write music. When he was unable to come up with anything, he did the rosary until he was able to find a melody to write. Leo Tolstoy wrote *War and Peace* seven times. Only those who have read this voluminous work of literature can truly appreciate that feat. Sir Isaac Newton, when working on a theory, was said to "keep the problem constantly before his mind." This is a trait that all successful artists and creative people embrace. They simply will not let the idea go away, and they are committed to subduing an idea before it subdues them.

Many aspiring writers, composers, artists, and others somehow mistakenly believe that there is an inspirational force that will descend upon them, making it possible for them to effortlessly bring forth an enduring masterpiece. Like anything else in life, once you know the true facts, you can count the cost and determine whether or not you want to pay the price.

I have been a successful athlete, investor, and entrepreneur, pursuing many endeavors, but I can honestly say that writing is one of the most difficult and rewarding things I have ever done. I do not like the process of writing, but I love the process of having written. Writing has been one of the greatest challenges and greatest gifts in my life. I hope you will make the commitment to pursue the passion in your life, and you just might change the world.

As you go through your day today, look for creative genius at the end of a lot of hard work.

***Today's the day!***

# NEW LIFE

NEW LIFE IS A POWERFUL CONCEPT AND POSSIBILITY IN
every area of our existence as well as the title of a new
movie that I am very proud to be associated with. (Visit: http://
bit.ly/NL_Order.) We can experience a new life in any aspect
of our world including our friends, our family, our faith, our
finances, or our fitness.

The first step to experiencing a new life is to release the old
life. Our world abhors a vacuum. Once you make space in any
area of your physical, mental, or spiritual life, something new
can fill that space, but it is impossible to get something for nothing. A seed must die for a new plant to grow. That plant will
bloom and create new seeds which, in turn, must die to keep the
cycle of growth and life moving ahead into the future.

The *New Life* movie concept came to me from an industry
colleague named Drew Waters. I met Drew when he was starring
in a movie based on my book *The Ultimate Life*. That movie
involved a flashback to follow the early life of Red Stevens who
may be the most iconic character I ever created in any of my
books. Red Stevens was played magnificently in *The Ultimate
Gift* by legendary actor James Garner, so the thought of having
someone else play that character as a younger man seemed awkward and uncomfortable to me. Then I met Drew Waters and

got to experience him bringing to life a younger version of the character that Mr. Garner had embodied in an earlier movie.

Drew and I were at a red carpet movie premiere event for *The Ultimate Life* when he turned to me and said, "I've got a story for a film that I've got to share with you." I was absolutely mesmerized by the story as you will be when you watch the *New Life* movie, but I was concerned when Drew told me he was not going to act in the film but would, instead, be making his directing debut on the project. My concerns were unfounded when I experienced the same energy Drew had brought to *The Ultimate Life* as an actor in every scene of the *New Life* movie as he directed it.

The film is a story of love, loss, legacy, learning, and experiencing new life. I am very pleased that my company, the Narrative Television Network, combined forces with Drew's production team so the 13 million blind and visually impaired Americans and their families as well as millions more around the world will be able to experience this powerful new movie.

I fervently hope you and your family will enjoy *New Life* as an entertaining movie experience, but also as a catalyst to reexamine your priorities and move to a higher level in every aspect of your existence.

As you go through your day today, leave the past behind, and step into a new life.

*Today's the day!*

# ELEVATING YOUR MIND

I'M A FIRM BELIEVER THAT WE ALL MOVE TOWARD OUR MOST immediate dominant thought, and we become what we think about all day. When I consider the news reports as well as the movies, television, and videogames that people allow to fill their minds, I'm actually surprised the world is as stable and well-functioning as it is.

We all understand the phrase "Garbage in, garbage out" because we know that the computers that run our personal and professional lives merely store and reconfigure the information that we input. There are so many informative, uplifting, and inspiring things in our world that there is no excuse for having a brain full of chaotic, pessimistic garbage.

Most of us live within a convenient driving distance from a public library. Most libraries today actually offer download-able selections online free-of-charge. Local colleges, universities, and civic organizations offer a number of informative cultural experiences and lectures. Even in the modern media amid the sea of mediocrity, there are many highly-educational and enlightening programs.

According to the American Alliance of Museums, there are approximately 850 million visits to American museums each year, more than all major league sporting events and theme parks combined. Over 2,000 museums offer free admission to active military personnel and their families, and many others offer free admission or deep discounts for children, students, and senior citizens.

There is simply no excuse for remaining ignorant or culturally deprived in our world today. Unfortunately, as a society, we are intellectually starving to death in the midst of the greatest intellectual and cultural smorgasbord the world has ever known.

I believe that the thing we measure is the thing that will move and grow. If you want to improve your physical fitness level, you need to be able to measure and monitor your diet and exercise. If you want to change your intellectual and cultural fitness, you need to begin to track and record your participation in the experiences that will bring you the results you seek. The act of simply putting a library visit or museum tour on your weekly calendar can begin to tip the scales in your favor as you reprogram your mind.

Change happens when we take control of our environment and current situation. You and I have more than enough resources to be informed, inspired, and enlightened.

In ancient times, the great library in Alexandria was located on the trade routes that connected Europe, Africa, and Asia. It was said that all the knowledge and the wisdom of the world was stored in that one location. The great library in Alexandria pales in comparison to the resources you and I have at our fingertips by accessing our computer, smart phone, or library card.

As you go through your day today, put your mind on a health food diet.

*Today's the day!*

# AGENDAS AND INFORMATION

**M**Y LATE, GREAT MENTOR LEE BRAXTON, WHO TAUGHT ME much of what I know about business, always said, "In every transaction or business deal, each party involved has an angle or motive." Mr. Braxton went on to explain that having an angle or a motive is actually positive, and any person you are dealing with who doesn't have an obvious angle or motive should be very suspect.

In a capitalistic, free enterprise system, profit motive and success angles are valid and important. In much the same way everyone in a business deal has a motive, everyone who offers you information has an agenda. It does not make their agenda bad or in any way antagonistic, but you must always remember that everyone who communicates with you has a reason or agenda for their communication.

My late, great friend and colleague Paul Harvey, arguably the most respected news professional of his time, told me that the way to control the flow of news is not to introduce your own bias into the story as much as deciding which stories will be told. By virtue of the fact that someone is telling you something, they are instantly communicating their belief that whatever they are telling you is worthy of your time and attention.

There was a time when all that anyone needed to discern from news or information was the simple question, "What is the story?" Then with the advent of numerous news and information sources, some being less than reputable, it became important to ask, "Who is telling the story?" Now with the world filled with a variety of individuals with differing agendas clamoring for our attention, it is important to ask ourselves, "Why are they telling me this story?"

Understanding a person's bias or agenda is the basis for very positive and constructive communication. It is impossible for anyone to be free of bias. Their experience and beliefs create the perspective from which they are communicating. You and I have biases and perspectives on everything around us. Often, the most honest communication begins with revealing our own bias, but just because someone doesn't reveal their bias or even admit that they have one, does not mean that there isn't a hidden bias or agenda.

When a salesperson calls on you, he has a bias toward his product and an agenda to sell it to you. A politician has a bias toward her position and an agenda to get your support. This is normal, healthy, and natural—until someone starts sharing questionable information with a hidden bias. Beware of anyone who doesn't seem to have a bias, a motive, or an agenda.

As you go through your day today, always be aware of your own bias, agenda, and motives as well as those of other people.

*Today's the day!*

# PREJUDICE AND PRIDE

A LL OF US WANT TO BE ACCEPTED AND VALUED BY THOSE around us. This acceptance is based upon other people's judgments. They can judge us on how we look, how we act, or how we perform.

Possibly the best way to judge and be judged came from Dr. Martin Luther King's powerful dream that his children be judged based on the "content of their character." This is a difficult judgment to make as it takes a lot of time, effort, and energy. Unfortunately, too many people in the world don't make the commitment to honestly judge everyone, and therefore, they engage in the practice of prejudging or prejudice. This is highly inaccurate, fallible, and dangerous. At its best, prejudice is a lazy mental shortcut.

I am a white, male, American who makes my home in Oklahoma. I am blind, I'm an author, I'm an entrepreneur, and I am a former Olympic weightlifting champion. Each of these individual elements and countless others can be the basis for someone to prejudge me. Their prejudice could be more favorable than I deserve or less favorable than I deserve but will rarely, if ever, be accurate.

Pride is how we judge ourselves. Much like our judgment of others, our judgment of ourselves is rarely authentic and accurate without a considerable amount of effort, energy, and contemplation. We can have pride in our accomplishments such as graduating from college; we can have pride in our affiliations such as being an American; or we can have pride in our associations such as our faith, family, and friends.

Having a proper amount of pride in these things can be very positive as we rarely outperform our own self-image; however, false pride is among the most damaging, debilitating, and destructive human emotions. When we engage in false pride, we often inaccurately compare ourselves to others or a distorted image of ourselves.

I find it highly beneficial if not imperative to have a trusted group of mentors, advisors, and accountability partners who help me to accurately judge myself and my performance. We can only be judged or judge ourselves against the image of who we know we should be based on our ability and our life goals.

When it comes to judging others, my late, great friend and mentor legendary Coach John Wooden often said, "There's enough good in the worst of us and enough bad in the best of us that it doesn't behoove any of us to judge anyone." I believe this is a standard worth aspiring to.

As you go through your day today, judge yourself with grace and everyone around you with mercy.

*Today's the day!*

# THE POWER OF PESSIMISM

OR SEVERAL DECADES, I HAVE ENDEAVORED TO CONVINCE people that having a positive attitude, focusing their energy, and acting upon their motivations can bring positive results in their lives and the people around them.

My late, great colleague, mentor, and friend Zig Ziglar was fond of saying, "I'm an optimist. I would go after Moby Dick in a rowboat and take the tartar sauce with me."

Unfortunately, our society seems to be predominantly populated by people who do not believe that being an optimist is worthwhile. Many of these individuals communicate to me that motivation and a positive attitude are just smoke and mirrors that might create temporary euphoria or warm, fuzzy feelings but don't really matter in the real world.

Sometimes it's easier to prove the opposite side of an argument. According to research conducted by Dr. Michael Scheier, "In general, pessimists don't perform as well in life as optimists. They tend to deny, avoid, and distort the problems they confront and dwell on their negative feelings." Dr. Scheier cites five specific scientifically provable results of being a pessimist:

1.  Pessimism kills your creativity. We always find what we're looking for, and pessimists seem to focus on negative results or nothing at all which does not promote innovative creative thinking. The research also

shows that pessimists hinder the creativity of colleagues, friends, and family members around them.

2. Pessimism harms you emotionally. The scientific study indicates that while motivation wears off and has to be renewed constantly, pessimism actually sticks with you and is reinforced when you have a fleeting negative thought. This brief shot of pessimism can instantly bring back all of the negative thoughts and emotions you have had and can stay with you long term.

3. Pessimism hurts you professionally. The statistics show that your attitude will affect your measurable performance on the job and will impact those around you negatively. This poor performance and bad attitude will keep you from promotions and bonuses while moving you ever closer to the unemployment line.

4. Pessimism damages relationships. Your friends and loved ones may not even directly notice your pessimism, but they will be aware of how they feel when they are around you or immediately after they have been in your presence. We subconsciously judge others by how they make us feel.

5. Pessimism makes you sick. You've heard of the placebo effect which causes people to get better because they think they're going to get better whether the treatment they are receiving is valid or not. The scientists studying pessimism came up with a term they call "nocebo" which, basically, indicates that if you think you're going to feel bad you will, and if you believe you're going to get sick, you will likely be

proven correct. The research went on to show that pessimism can lead directly to heart attacks and other serious problems including dementia.

If I haven't convinced you to be an optimist yet, I hope the current scientific research will at least motivate you to stop being a pessimist.

As you go through your day today, avoid the power of pessimism—be optimistic and live well.

*Today's the day!*

# GRACE AND MERCY

TWO OF THE MOST MISUNDERSTOOD WORDS AND CONCEPTS in our society today are grace and mercy. While some people use the terms almost interchangeably, they are quite different concepts and almost opposite in some ways. Grace means we receive something to which we are not entitled. Mercy means that we avoid a penalty that we deserve. Ideally, we should give and receive both grace and mercy.

Unfortunately, the media's ability to microscopically examine a single element of any person's life, makes the application of grace and mercy difficult. Left to our own perspective, we all have a tendency to judge everyone else's performance while judging our own intentions. This gives us a myopic, self-centered view of the world.

If you or I are late to a meeting, our internal and even our external dialogue often goes something like, "Well, I meant to be on time. I'm almost always on time. And besides that, I left early enough to make it, but no one can anticipate bad traffic, road construction, and out-of-order elevators. Everyone will just have to deal with it."

If someone else, on the other hand, is late for a meeting and they keep us waiting, our internal and possibly our external dialogue will be more like, "I don't know why they can't get here on time. This meeting has been set for weeks, and two o'clock means two o'clock. No excuses."

The most well-known philosopher of his time, Will Rogers, who was a Cherokee Indian, was fond of saying, "You can't judge anyone unless you've walked a mile in their moccasins." It was this kind of nonjudgmental grace and mercy perspective that made Will's most popular quote a reality for him and a possibility for the rest of us. "I never met a man I didn't like."

Will Rogers traveled around the world at a time when aviation was in its infancy, and few people had seen as many cultures and countries as he had. Will Rogers met world leaders and experienced the Great Depression and world war. He was very positive and optimistic but never naïve. He found many things about many people to be objectionable and even deplorable, but he was still willing to not judge others without considering their perspective, and he was left with his own conviction that— judged on the whole—he never met a man he didn't like.

We must all strive to disagree without being disagreeable, and debate the value of issues and not the worth of people. Gandhi told us that every person is our superior in that we can learn something from them. Therein lies the beginning of grace and mercy.

As you go through your day today, practice grace and mercy with other people and the whole world.

*Today's the day!*

# WILL AND WILL

IHAVE HAD THE PRIVILEGE OF WRITING WEEKLY COLUMNS FOR 20 years. *Winners' Wisdom* began in a local business journal in my hometown and has expanded to newspapers, magazines, and online publications literally around the world. It is read by several million people each week, and I am grateful for their and your interest and support.

Writing a regular column is an ongoing balance between information and opinion. I always seek to be factual, but I share *Winners' Wisdom* from my own perspective, which is the only one I have to share. Whether you agree with me or not, I hope *Winners' Wisdom* causes you to think and act. On the occasions we might disagree, please remember it's only my opinion, and I am still the world's leading authority on my opinion.

In order to improve my skills and perspective as a columnist, I have read countless columns written by a myriad of writers. In the world of columnists, it seems to me that two individuals rise above the crowd in both their expertise and their impact.

The most influential columnist of his time and possibly any time was Will Rogers. Will is the favorite son of my home state of Oklahoma. He wrote a daily column for many years. This was long before the Internet and the high-speed transmission of digital data. Will Rogers' columns were typed on a manual typewriter and transmitted via telegraph from coast to coast and beyond every day.

There was a question that many Americans greeted one another with during the 1920s and 1930s. Much like we might ask, "How are you doing?" they asked one another, "Have you read Will yet today?" Before the Internet and network television, Will Rogers was the glue that held our country together.

Among the columnists working today, George Will could be considered a giant. You don't have to always agree with George's opinion to respect his perspective and his presentation. George is fond of saying, "You cannot reason people out of a position they did not reason themselves into."

Before you try to change someone's opinion based on the height of your logic, up-to-the-minute statistics, or the facts as you see them, determine whether they are holding their current opinion based on emotion or reason. People who have come to their conclusions solely based on emotion will not change their minds regardless of facts, logic, or current reality.

Before you engage in any dialogue or debate, determine whether you are arguing against reason or emotion. I have held a number of opinions that I came to via logic or statistics. I am perfectly willing to change my opinion if and when the facts change; however, there are other opinions I hold based on emotion. These opinions are very personal to me, and cannot be so easily altered.

As you go through your day today, determine whether you're dealing with emotion or reason before you discuss or debate.

*Today's the day!*

# THE ART OF PRESENTATION

E VERY GREAT PROFESSIONAL UNDERSTANDS THE DIFFERENCE between information and presentation. We all live in the information age and regularly deal with the advantages and the challenges that it offers us. If you only want to deliver information, a memo, email, or even a text may suffice, but if you want to deliver emotion, attitudes, and impact, you need to employ the art of presentation.

I am very proud, along with my esteemed coauthor Dr. Raymond Hull, of our book *The Art of Presentation*. (Visit www. JimStovallBooks.com.) As a professional speaker for more than a quarter of a century, I've come to realize that corporations and associations regularly pay me a considerable amount of money to deliver a small fraction of the material that is contained in just one of my 30-plus books. Obviously, they want more than mere facts or simple information. They want impact, emotion, and a memorable catalyst for change.

If we were to take William Shakespeare's masterpiece, *Romeo and Juliet,* and reduce it to information, it might look something like "boy meets girl, their families disagree, tragedy ensues." The difference between this terse phrase and Mr. Shakespeare's enduring work of art is the difference between information and presentation.

I've had the privilege of having six of my books turned into major motion pictures with several others in production at this writing. The difference between simple words on a page and emotion impactfully exploding on the silver screen illustrates the contrast between information and presentation; however, great writers—like great professionals—can turn their information into an unforgettable presentation.

Simple phrases such as "Go ahead, make my day," "Toto, I have a feeling we're not in Kansas anymore," "Here's lookin' at you, kid," or "May the Force be with you," are not just communicating information. They are indelibly etched into the fabric of our society. One powerfully-presented idea or concept can be a transformational experience in a person's career or their life.

As a young man, my only ambition in life was to be an All-American football player and then make my living playing in the NFL. The coaches and scouts who evaluate players assured me that I had the size, speed, and talent to make my dreams a reality. Then, one year during a routine physical in preparation to play another season of football, I was diagnosed with the condition that would cause me to lose my sight. My dreams were shattered, and I did, indeed, completely lose my sight by age 29.

Many things contributed to my rehabilitation and the life I know today, but if I were to pick one transformational, fork-in-the-road turning point, it would have been listening to an audiotape of the bestselling author Dr. Denis Waitley. I wasn't worried about making a living or living a normal life, I was simply wondering if I could ever get out of my little 9- by 12-foot room and walk the 50 feet to my mailbox. I sat for many days simply contemplating the overwhelming prospect of traversing those 50 feet down my driveway to the mailbox at the curb. As a totally-blind person with no skills, it seemed impossible, but on that tape, Dr. Waitley offered more than information. He delivered a powerful presentation of the phrase "If you think you can, you can."

This may seem overly simplistic as all great truths do, but when powerful ideas come to life in transformational presentations, they change people who can, in turn, change the world. If we are to create these powerful presentations, we must, as my late, great friend and colleague Stephen Covey told us, "Begin with the end in mind."

If you know the emotion, attitudes, or change you want to come from any presentation, you can make it a reality.

*Today's the day!*

# CONCERN AND WORRY

ORRY IS A DESTRUCTIVE EMOTION THAT CAN CAUSE US TO
be unhappy, depressed, and physically ill. Concern is a
positive emotion that helps us focus on people and situations
where we can make a difference. If worry causes failure and
concern can create success, it becomes imperative that we understand the difference.

Worry is an exercise in futility involving fretting over things
in which we have no control. My airline statement tells me
that I have flown over 2 million miles, which is more than 80
times around the world. This is hard to believe and makes me
exhausted just thinking about it. People often ask if I am worried about the risk of flying. Statistics show us that flying on
a commercial airliner is one of the most safe and secure activities in which we can engage. There is more risk in driving to
your local airport than flying around the world; however, if you
unduly worry about flying, it can make you depressed and sick.
Unreasonable worry about airline travel can keep you from experiencing the whole world.

I do not worry about air travel because there is nothing I can
do about the weather, the mechanical operation of the plane, or
the activities of the pilot. I simply have no control, and therefore,
if I focus on the dangers involved, I am experiencing worry and
not concern. I can be concerned about getting to the airport on
time, booking the best flights and connections, or selecting the

best route of travel for the seasonal weather conditions. These are aspects of airline travel that are under my control.

I spoke with a gentleman who was worried about the corporation he works for failing, and therefore, leaving him unemployed. He works for a multibillion dollar, multinational organization. There is nothing his worry can do to impact his fate, but if he would be concerned about updating his resume, renewing his career contacts, and learning about the latest cutting-edge developments in his field, he can take control of the uncertainty.

I don't mean to imply that there aren't frightening things in the world, but if we can take control of our emotions, eliminating worry when there's nothing we can do, and focus our concerns on elements we can change, we can feel empowered and move forward instead of being paralyzed with fear and worry.

As you go through your day today, eliminate worry and focus your concern.

*Today's the day!*

# THE REUNIONS

IATTENDED TWO VERY SIGNIFICANT REUNIONS: MY ANNUAL family reunion and my 40th high school reunion. Many people avoid the reunions in their lives thinking they are boring, awkward, or irrelevant.

One of the best definitions I've ever heard of living a successful life admonishes us to "Make great memories." If you and I are, indeed, going to invest our time, effort, and energy in making great memories, we should periodically pause to reflect, remember, and savor the memories we've made.

I come from a very small extended family as my father is an only child, and my mother grew up in a family having only two siblings. A number of years ago, my cousin Steve contacted all the cousins in our family and organized an annual family reunion. Each spring, our family travels from various points across the country—and even overseas—to meet at Bridgeport Resort on Table Rock Lake in southern Missouri. It is three days of fun, food, and family. We are a diverse group of people, and sometimes it seems the only thing we have in common is our roots, but roots give us the background and foundation of who we are and what we can become.

I remember going to family reunions as a child and sometimes being bored with elderly grandparents or great aunts and uncles I couldn't relate to. Today, I would give a small fortune to get to spend an hour with those people.

Our family reunion has grown to include a number of friends and neighbors who simply like to join in our celebration. Our world is filled with some people who have no family or come from backgrounds that are painful and destructive.

In my book and the subsequent movie titled *The Ultimate Gift*, I described family by stating: "Some people are born into wonderful families. Others have to find or create them. Being a member of a family is a priceless membership that we pay nothing for but love."

For many people, including myself, high school was a mixed blessing, and not all of the memories are pleasant ones, but reconnecting with classmates throughout the years is a great perspective upon who we were, what we've become, and how we might maximize our future. People with whom we have shared our past can help us understand the present and view the future. Like many things in this life, if you will think about reunions as a way to give back and reconnect instead of what you might initially enjoy or get out of it, you will discover the hidden blessing.

As you go through your day today, remember the past and celebrate your family.

*Today's the day!*

# IT'S ON THE LABEL

I BELIEVE IN TODAY'S SOCIETY WE HAVE MORE INFORMATION and less common sense than any generation that has gone before us. Benjamin Franklin told us that common sense is not very common. If that was true in Ben's day, it certainly must apply to us. We are overloaded and bombarded with countless messages and instructions each day. Many of these messages yield to the lowest common denominator among us. There are some things in this life we should endeavor to change. Others we should strive to accept, and some things we should just laugh at.

I like to consider myself a fairly creative writer, but you can't make this stuff up. The following are printed instructions that actually appeared on packaging for consumer items.

On a hairdryer: Do not use while sleeping.

On a bag of corn chips: You could be a winner! No purchase necessary. Details inside.

On a bar of soap: Directions—Use like regular soap.

On a frozen dinner: Serving suggestion—defrost.

On a hotel shower cap: Fits one head!

On the bottom of a dessert box: Do not turn upside down.

On a pudding box: Product will be hot after heating.

On a label of an electric iron: Do not iron clothes on body!

On a package of children's cough medicine: Do not drive car or operate machinery.

On the package of a sleeping pill: Warning—may cause drowsiness.

On a label on a kitchen knife: Warning—keep out of children.

On a string of Christmas lights: For indoor or outdoor use only.

On a food processor label: Not to be used for the other use.

On a can of peanuts: Warning! Contains nuts.

On a chainsaw label: Do not attempt to stop chain with your hands!

On an airline package of peanuts: Instructions— Open packet. Eat nuts.

The serious fact about absurd and even comical instructions is that they cause us to question the validity of everything surrounding the product, service, or people involved.

In my book, *The Art of Communication*, my coauthor Dr. Ray Hull and I explore the difference between what we meant to say, what we intended to say, and what we actually said. You can access a sample of the eBook or audiobook version of *The Art of Communication* at www.JimStovallBooks.com.

If you don't think these kinds of things matter or stay with us, just ask Dan Quayle about potatoes.

As you go through your day today, heed wise instructions, laugh at others, and watch what you say.

*Today's the day!*

# CHANGING YOUR MIND

I'M A FIRM BELIEVER THAT YOU CAN CHANGE YOUR LIFE WHEN you change your mind. Your mind is the most powerful tool you have. We have the ability to accumulate information and then utilize that information to make a decision.

I am saddened to encounter people who came in contact with some information many years ago and made up their minds about something to an extent they are not open to more information. You should always be accumulating new facts and more information and continually challenging past beliefs.

C. S. Lewis said, "Every conversion begins with blessed defeat." There was a time when the smartest people in the world, utilizing the best information of the day, were convinced that the world was flat. They staunchly held this belief for many years; but thankfully, some enlightened individuals were willing to risk the scorn and ridicule of others as they gained more information and changed their minds.

While there is virtue in holding a consistent belief over a long period of time, there is more virtue in challenging your beliefs, being willing to change, and therefore, being right. Whether it's the flat earth, slavery, economic views, or political beliefs, we advance when we re-examine and challenge past thoughts in the light of new information.

The most important beliefs we hold are those things we believe about ourselves. The history books are full of slaves who became kings, paupers who became wealthy, and timid souls who became great leaders who changed the world. These individuals did not change their worldview until they changed their internal view.

I read a story once about an eaglet that somehow got mixed in with a group of baby ducks. The eaglet grew and learned about the world around him from the perspective of a duck. This continued until the day the eaglet looked far up into the sky and saw a full-grown bald eagle soaring majestically on the wind. The eaglet no longer saw himself as a duck and lived out the rest of his life as an eagle. The world around him had not changed, but he caught a new vision of who he was and who he could be.

I would challenge you to examine every area of the life you are living now, and determine whether you need to change your mind about who you are and become who you were meant to be.

As you go through your day today, remember you can change your life when you change your mind.

*Today's the day!*

# Fourth Time's a Charm

A S WE APPROACHED THE 1,000TH EDITION OF *WINNERS'*
*Wisdom*, my publisher, in conjunction with The Napoleon
Hill Foundation, released a third compilation volume of these
columns titled *Wisdom for Winners Volume 3*. (Visit: www.
JimStovallBooks.com.)

You are now holding the fourth volume, and the proceeds
from this new book and the three previous are being donated to
The Napoleon Hill Foundation to support their ongoing work to
extend the legacy and impact of Napoleon Hill and the message
of *Think and Grow Rich*. Napoleon Hill was born in the 19th century, changed the world in the 20th century, and now his timeless
message is the basis for many exciting new books, movies, and
success tools. A new book and movie project will be released
in 2017 titled *Top of the Hill*, which is part of my *Homecoming
Historical Series* focusing on great people from the past who lived
their lives in such a manner that we can use their example as a
way to build our own future.

We become what we think about all day, and unfortunately,
we are bombarded constantly with negative, distracting, and
even destructive messages. Technology has opened the whole
world to us, but it has also created the need for everyone to
control the input that goes into our minds. If you simply let
the media, the Internet, and program producers have free

rein in your environment, your likelihood of success will be virtually eliminated.

Our minds are the greatest creation we have to change the world and shape our own lives, but like any other vehicle, your mind is subject to the fuel you put into it. If you put contaminated gasoline in your car, it will begin to run poorly and eventually will stop running at all. If you allow contaminated thoughts to enter your mind, it will cease to function as a vehicle to reach your goals.

The columns I write each week are designed to give readers some positive thoughts. They are not necessarily my thoughts, but hopefully they will become your thoughts. As a columnist, I have discovered that it is not my job to give you answers; but instead, it is my job to frame the questions for which you already have innate answers that will get you from where you are to where you want to be. I am very proud that my columns are now not only available around the world each week but are as close as your bookshelf or eReader where you can access *Wisdom for Winners 1, 2,* and *3.*

 Your mind will take you anywhere you want to go if you just keep your tank filled with powerful, positive, and impactful fuel.

As you go through your day today, eliminate contamination and fill up with *Wisdom for Winners.*

**Today's the day!**

# TIME AND TRADITIONS

# Worth a Thousand Words

AS THE AUTHOR OF NUMEROUS BOOKS, I HAVE COME TO REAL-
ize that in spite of wise advice to the contrary, we do indeed
judge books by their covers. As a blind person, I find this to be
humorous, perplexing, and a bit disturbing. I realize that millions
of people around the world will read these words in newspapers,
magazines, and online publications, but to me, the words you are
reading on a page or computer screen are merely thoughts that I
dictated to my talented colleague Dorothy Thompson who for-
mulated them into words, sentences, and paragraphs that were
electronically transmitted around the world.

Whether we're selecting an automobile, a suit of clothes, or
a political candidate, the overall tendency is to allow the visual
impression to greatly impact our judgment. How something
looks can be an indicator of its depth and substance, but rarely
does it tell the whole story.

Every few days, I enjoy having a lengthy phone conversation with my brother who lives in another state. Last week, he
described a picture to me that he had seen online and asked me
for my best guess that might explain what he was looking at.
The picture shows a very mature tree, which is probably three
feet in diameter or even larger. Approximately four feet off the
ground, a bicycle is protruding from the trunk of the tree. On
one side of the tree, the front wheel and handlebars appear to

be growing out of the middle of the trunk; and protruding from the other side of the tree, the back wheel and fender of the bike can be seen.

My first thought was that it was some sort of optical illusion or Photoshop prank. Then I imagined someone had cut a bicycle in half and somehow attached it to either side of the tree. Finally, I gave up guessing, and my brother read me the brief message on a sign that explained the picture and forever changed my perspective. The sign reads, "In 1914, a young man chained his bicycle to this tree and went off to serve in World War I. He never returned." Instantly, my mental image changed from something comical or absurd to something profound and deeply moving.

A picture can, indeed, be worth a thousand or many thousands of words. I have had the privilege of having six of my novels being turned into movies, and the brief, flickering images on the screen can often deliver indelible concepts and impactful messages far beyond mere words.

As you go through your day today, look beyond what you're seeing, and discover your vision.

*Today's the day!*

# WISDOM IN THE FISH TANK

M Y LATE, GREAT FRIEND AND COLLEAGUE DR. STEPHEN
Covey was among the most influential writers, speakers,
and thought leaders of our time. His book, _First Things First_,
should be required reading for anyone wanting to succeed in
business or in life.

Here in the 21st century, we are bombarded with opportunities
to spend our time doing all manner of things. Some are productive, and others are not. In order to know if we are spending our
time wisely, we must know what return we hope to get from any
investment of time as time is more precious than money or any
other commodity because it can never be replaced or recaptured.

I shared the stage on several occasions with Dr. Covey,
and he was fond of using an object lesson demonstrated by an
audience member to make a memorable impression. Dr. Covey
would bring an empty 20-gallon fish tank onto the stage. It was
a four-sided glass rectangle, so it was obvious to everyone present
that there was nothing in the tank.

He picked a volunteer from the audience and asked her to
fill the tank using rocks that were about the size of softballs
and were piled up near the fish tank. The audience volunteer
dutifully placed the rocks into the fish tank filling it to the top.
When it was clear that she couldn't get one more rock into the
tank, Dr. Covey asked a simple but profound question. "Is the

tank full?" The volunteer from the audience and the rest of the crowd agreed that the tank was completely full.

Dr. Covey then handed the volunteer a bucket filled with gravel and asked her to pour the gravel into the tank. Two and one-half buckets later, the gravel filled the tank to the top. Dr. Covey then asked another poignant question. "Obviously the tank wasn't filled before, but is it full now?" Just as everyone agreed the tank was completely full, Dr. Covey handed the volunteer from the audience a bucket of sand and asked her to pour it into the tank. Several buckets of sand were emptied into the fish tank before the sand reached the top. Dr. Covey inquired again, "So now, is the fish tank full?" The audience members, seeing the fish tank filled with sand, all agreed that the fish tank was completely full, and nothing else would fit inside.

Then Dr. Covey handed the audience volunteer a bucket of water and asked her to pour it into the tank. After several buckets were poured into the fish tank, the water reached the top level, clearly demonstrating that although on several occasions the fish tank appeared to be completely full, it was not.

Dr. Covey then brought out another empty fish tank and asked the volunteer to fill it again, but change the order so the water would go in first, followed by the sand, then the gravel, and finally the rocks. It rapidly became obvious to everyone there that in order to get the maximum amount in the fish tank, the tank must be filled in the right order. In this way, Dr. Covey demonstrated one of the most powerful time management and success tools of all time. "Do the right thing next and the next thing right."

As you go through your day today, remember the wisdom that can be held within a fish tank.

*Today's the day!*

# New Solutions to
# Old Problems

IT SEEMS AS THOUGH WE ARE FACING MORE WORLDWIDE problems than ever before. While this may be true, I suspect much of the crisis consciousness is a result of the speed and availability of news reporting and communications around the world.

If we were to look back at some of the overwhelming problems of the 20th century, they simply don't exist anymore. In the early portion of the last century, global pandemic threats of polio, whooping cough, and diphtheria had many experts proclaiming that human survivability to the end of the 20th century was in doubt. In the mid-20th century, the energy crisis and surrounding publicity would have had us thinking that the world would go dark long before the new millennium, and recent health scares such as Ebola, killer bees, SARS, and even AIDS have proven to be manageable.

The speed of innovation that we are facing today is unprecedented and exciting, but must be factored into everything we do. People under 40 years of age who are working today are likely employed in a career that will be obsolete before they retire. The arenas of bioinformatics, biotechnology, nanotechnology, robotics, and neurosciences are changing the landscape and altering the future. Many jobs that we grew up believing would always require a human to perform are destined to be eliminated by robots, computers, and emerging technologies. While the initial reaction to change is often fear, we must look beyond the frightening aspects of these developments and consider the possibilities.

Many of the diseases we know today will not exist a generation from now. When the human elements are diminished or removed from driving a vehicle, one of the major causes of early death can be eliminated. Those who will succeed in this brave new world are those who do not avoid change but embrace it and even get out in front of it. Those enlightened individuals who can view the future as a master views the chessboard, will think several moves ahead and be ready to profit and succeed as innovation proliferates.

While jobs and whole industries will be eliminated in the coming decades, new careers and entire fields of study and industry will be created. The only absolute we can count on is change. We can never feel as if we have learned all we need to know or mastered our area of expertise because in the unlikely event we momentarily reach that mountaintop, we will discover that the mountain is growing, and new mountain ranges are forming in the distance.

In the final analysis, whether you believe these developments will be good for you or bad for you, you are right.

As you go through your day today, believe that the best is yet to come.

*Today's the day!*

# WHEN OPPORTUNITY KNOCKS

GREAT OPPORTUNITIES MAY SEEM SOLID AND TIMELESS LIKE a beautiful diamond, but they are often fragile and fleeting like an orchid.

Victor Hugo is known for having written great statements of wisdom. Among them is his admonition, "Nothing is more powerful than an idea whose time has come." It is important to realize that Victor Hugo's statement contains two variables: the idea and the timing.

I have met several sad individuals who—upon encountering a bestselling book, new business success, or dynamic invention— have gone back into their files and shown me that they had the same idea or concept years or even decades earlier. While it is true that nothing is more powerful than an idea whose time has come, the idea must be implemented or acted upon; otherwise it is powerless and insignificant.

Timing has absolute worth and value. You can buy and sell options on almost any financial instrument, real estate, or commodity in the world's marketplaces and various exchanges. People will pay you for the opportunity to buy something or sell it at a future date. They're not paying for the investment. They're paying for the time. At the end of that option, it expires and becomes worthless. Your ideas and thoughts are much the same. If you act on them, you may change the world. If you sit on them, they may become worthless in the coming days and months.

I clearly remember the day a gentleman approached me with a unique design for a new type of mechanic's wrench. While I have little or no knowledge of tools, I do know one of the leading patent attorneys in the country. I promptly called him, and since he was a friend, he was willing to meet with us at his home on a weekend. I accompanied the gentleman with his prototype wrench to the patent lawyer's home, and we were welcomed into his study. The gentleman proudly showed the patent attorney the wrench he had designed, and the attorney began laughing uncontrollably. I was about to question his rude and insensitive response when he reached into a desk drawer and took out a shiny carrying case that he opened to reveal a set of wrenches virtually identical to the one that the gentleman had brought. The attorney explained that he had done the patent work for these revolutionary new wrenches three years earlier, and the new wrenches had made his client very wealthy.

The gentleman who had accompanied me to the attorney's home dejectedly tossed his prototype into a trash can beside the attorney's desk and muttered that he'd had the prototype sitting in the back of his drawer for more than 15 years. Whenever confronted by an idea, concept, or inspiration, remember the Latin phrase *Carpe diem*, and seize the day.

As you go through your day today, remember ideas come to us for a reason and for a season.

*Today's the day!*

# FREE ICE CREAM

DIGITAL DEVICES MAKE GREAT SLAVES BUT POOR MASTERS. I have a friend named Arthur Greeno who owns several *Chick-fil-A* locations in my hometown. Arthur told me about a promotion they are running that provides free ice cream for any family dining in the restaurant who will all put away their digital devices throughout the meal. My first thought was this is a catchy and appealing promotion, but then the hidden and looming danger in our overall society began to dawn on me.

It is sad and disappointing that we have devolved to a point where families have to be bribed with ice cream to sit and talk at the dinner table. While I applaud Arthur and *Chick-fil-A* for this initiative, it speaks ill of us all that such a promotion is even relevant.

My wife, Crystal, and I have celebrated more than 35 years together. We remain happily married and best friends in great part due to consistent communication. We both have busy lives and heavy, independent travel schedules, but we spend time each day catching up and staying current on one another's activities, goals, and passions.

I'm a very early riser and get up each day at 4 a.m. to begin my reading, study, and planning for the day. Crystal, who is not naturally a morning person, has made the ongoing commitment to get up at 6 a.m. so we can spend an hour together by the fire or out in the garden, depending on the season, to simply talk. Sometimes we discuss our schedules or plans for the day while other times we discuss current events and issues in the news. The things we focus on are the things in our lives that are going to improve.

I heard a staggering statistic that in the average American home, the television is on for more than seven hours each day—yet the average parent spends less than an hour a week in focused, uninterrupted conversation with their children. Whether it's friends, colleagues, or your spouse, all significant relationships begin with conversation, and it is that ongoing interaction and dialogue that will maintain those relationships.

I am very grateful that as I approach another birthday, both of my parents are still productive and active for people in their mid-80s. Several years ago, it dawned on me that although my parents live approximately three miles from my home, I hadn't seen them in several months. We talked regularly on the phone, but that seemed to be a poor substitute for family interaction, so we started our Friday night family dinner tradition. Every Friday night, travel schedules permitting, my mom and dad come to our house for dinner. It has become one of my favorite times of the week, and though we often enjoy dessert, I'm pleased to report we don't have to bribe anyone with ice cream to put away our digital devices and focus on family.

As you go through your day today, control your technology and don't let it control you.

*Today's the day!*

# FACTS, THEORIES, AND OPINIONS

WE TRULY LIVE IN THE INFORMATION AGE. OUR ANCESTORS would be amazed at the amount of data that is readily available at our fingertips; however, all information is not created equal.

My good friend and colleague, Dr. Michael Johnson, said, "Not knowing how to do something rarely stops anyone from giving advice on it."

With the proliferation of the Internet, blogs, and podcasts, anyone can get a following and gather an audience. As I often tell my colleagues in the professional speaking industry, just because you're holding a microphone doesn't mean you have anything worth saying, and just because you're standing in a spotlight doesn't make you bright.

I read a book by the late Benjamin Bradlee who was editor of *The Washington Post* during the Watergate years. Bradlee grew up during the generation that saw newsmen like Edward R. Murrow and Walter Cronkite. There were certain standards that were understood by most everyone in the news and information profession. People were more interested in being right than being first. Today, you can put something out on the Internet, and within a few moments, other people around the world will be quoting you. It's important that we know the original source of information if we are going to accept it as true and act upon it.

My late great friend and colleague Paul Harvey had a daily broadcast heard by people across the country and, literally, around the world. He titled his broadcast *Paul Harvey News and Comment*. Mr. Harvey was very particular about separating the news from his own commentary.

Information can be divided into three categories: facts, theories, and opinions. To be considered a fact, something should be provable, repeatable, and verifiable; however, experts can disagree on facts, and even if something is a fact today, it may be disproved tomorrow.

Theories are facts that have been stretched to an unprovable or unknown conclusion. Based on something being true here and now, a theory might conclude the same truth elsewhere or at a different time. Theories are useful, but they should always be challenged, and the underlying facts must be constantly checked.

Opinions are nothing more or less than someone's thoughts. They can be rooted in facts and theories or may simply be random. Opinions should always be labeled. The premise "in my opinion" makes virtually any statement valid. I may know anything or nothing about a certain topic, but I am still entitled to my opinion. It's important to point out here that I am still the world's leading authority on my opinion—as you are on your opinion—but we must remember to be clear when something is merely our opinion as opposed to a theory or a fact.

You should never make a decision without information, but before you leap, find out whether you're acting upon facts, theories, or just someone's opinion.

As you go through your day today, seek information but question it carefully.

***Today's the day!***

# YOUR HOUSE, YOUR STREET

THE 2016 PRESIDENTIAL ELECTION IN THE UNITED STATES was a long, grueling, and painful process much like childbirth, but it offered great promise and wonderful opportunities much like having a new baby in the house.

Whether you were pleased or disappointed with the results of the election, it's important to remember that the process worked, and now we are all on the same team. Much like the verdict rendered in a courtroom, the conflict can bring clarity and truth into the light of day.

For those who campaigned and voted, believing that government is going to solve all their problems, I hate to be the one to bring the bad news, but government rarely, if ever, creates the outcomes we seek; but instead, government at its best clears the way and gives us a track to run on so we can create the outcomes we want in our lives. If you watch the news regularly, you might assume that what happens in the White House and on Wall Street controls your life. In reality, what happens in your house and on your street is what makes the difference.

A great statesman once said, "A government that can give you anything you want can take away everything you have."

If you campaigned and voted in the 2016 election, you are to be applauded whether your candidate was victorious or not. You participated in the process and exercised your hard-won and cherished right to choose. From this point forward, we all need to hold government accountable and make our own lives the success that we and our families deserve.

We are fortunate to have a government of the people, by the people, and for the people. If we don't like the leadership we have or the policies that exist, we need to seek to change them as we seek to change and improve our own lives. A government that is $20 trillion in debt can't create wealth for its citizens, but it can clear the way so you can create your own success.

Our founding documents declare that we are entitled to life, liberty, and the pursuit of happiness. This means we need to control our own destiny and call upon our government to clear the way so every person has the maximum opportunity to achieve the highest level of life, liberty, and happiness.

Equal opportunity does not mean equal results. Freedom allows us all to visualize our own success and pursue our own destiny.

As you go through your day today, let government maintain the track so you and I can race to the finish line.

*Today's the day!*

# PERSPECTIVES FROM THE PAST

THE MEDIA AND THE INTERNET BOMBARD US WITH DIRE predictions countless times each day. It sometimes seems everyone we encounter is preaching gloom and doom, so every once in a while, it's good to bring a little sanity into our lives by introducing perspectives from the past.

In 1955, our parents or grandparents would have heard the following statements from the media or people they encountered:

- Did you hear the post office is thinking about charging 7 cents just to mail a letter?

- If they raise the minimum wage to $1.00, nobody will be able to hire outside help at the store.

- When I first started driving, who would have thought gas would someday cost 25 cents a gallon? Guess we'd be better off leaving the car in the garage.

- Did you see where some baseball player just signed a contract for $50,000 a year just to play ball? It wouldn't surprise me if someday they'll be making more than the president.

- It's too bad things are so tough nowadays. I see where a few married women are having to work to make ends meet.

- It won't be long before young couples are going to have to hire someone to watch their kids so they can both work.

- I'm afraid the Volkswagen car is going to open the door to a whole lot of foreign business.

- Thank goodness I won't live to see the day when the government takes half our income in taxes. I sometimes wonder if we are electing the best people to government.

- The fast food restaurant is convenient for a quick meal, but I seriously doubt they will ever catch on.

- There is no sense going on short trips any more for a weekend. It costs nearly $2.00 a night to stay in a hotel.

- No one can afford to be sick any more. At $15.00 a day in the hospital, it's too rich for my blood.

- If they think I'll pay 30 cents for a haircut, forget it.

It's important for us to remember that the pessimists are generally wrong, and the optimists are usually right. If you maintain a good attitude and share it with everyone around you, you will be proven right most of the time, and you will enjoy a far better life as you encounter the nay-sayers in the media or in person.

We can never control the things around us, but we can always control our attitude. Ironically, whether you believe your future will be bright or you believe you are facing bad days ahead, you are inevitably right.

As you go through your day today, remember the past and look forward to a bright future.

*Today's the day!*

# A Paid-Off Debt

L IKE MILLIONS OF PEOPLE AROUND THE WORLD, I ENJOY watching the Masters Golf Tournament. Each year the greatest golfers around the globe descend upon the Augusta National Golf Course for arguably the greatest tournament in the world. Masters week signals that springtime is in full bloom, and the golf tradition is enduring.

Among the great Masters traditions is the ceremonial drive on the first tee. This involves legendary champions gathering to hit the first shot off of the first tee that signals the beginning of the tournament. For a number of years, three legendary champions—Arnold Palmer, Jack Nicklaus, and Gary Player—have come together in this historic ceremony.

One year Arnold Palmer announced that he would not be participating in the first drive. He was the beloved leader of his legion of fans known around the world as *Arnie's Army*, and they were obviously disappointed, as it signaled the end of an era. One misguided and possibly delusional reporter criticized Arnold Palmer for not hitting the first drive. This reporter was actually heard to say, "Arnold Palmer owes the public and should participate."

I want to clearly say that Arnold Palmer owed the public, his fans, and the game of golf absolutely nothing. Golf made Arnold

Palmer wealthy, famous, and a worldwide celebrity, but he gave far more back to the game and the world than he ever took away.

I have had the great fortune of interviewing the other two longtime participants in the ceremonial first drive at the Masters. Both Jack Nicklaus and Gary Player have participated in several of my book projects, and I am humbled that Jack Nicklaus is an avid reader of my books including several compilations of *Winners' Wisdom* columns you are reading.

Both Nicklaus and Player gave credit to Arnold Palmer for elevating the game of golf to a level where they both could compete, win, and prosper. Arnold Palmer was a success in golf, business, and life. Part of being a great competitor is knowing when to get off the field of play. Arnold Palmer definitely doesn't need me to speak for him, but I'm certain he wanted to be known and remembered for the great champion he was and not for hitting a poor ceremonial drive in his late 80s, far beyond the point where his body could respond to his champion's mind and spirit.

I know that someday Jack Nicklaus and Gary Player will come to the same fork in the road as Arnold Palmer did. At that point, they will find that Arnie not only paved the way for their success throughout their careers, but he showed them the way to exit the stage with grace and dignity.

Every competitor, myself included, is convinced that he or she has one more championship performance in them. It takes a true competitor to step aside, leave your legacy as you built it, and move into the next phase of your life. Arnold Palmer was a leader, a role model, and a champion during his life—and far beyond.

As you go through your day today, remember Arnold Palmer and build your own legacy.

*Today's the day!*

# SOCIALISM SEDUCTION

**M**Y WEEKLY COLUMN, FROM WHICH THIS BOOK IS DERIVED, is read literally around the world each week, and the U.S. political news coverage has become global. U.S. election landscapes have begun to resemble a schoolyard brawl, a circus, or a gossip column. Democracy can be a bit like sausage in that the final result may be enjoyable, but the process can be unpleasant.

During each presidential election, it is important to remember that something rare and precious happens. The current leader of the free world, arguably the most powerful person on earth, voluntarily abandons this lofty office and turns it over to an individual selected by *We, the People.*

A recent campaign had several notable undercurrents. Among them were issues surrounding socialism. It would be difficult for many of our ancestors to imagine that an American presidential campaign would include elements of socialism within the rhetoric and debate.

America has become the most dominant and benevolent nation on earth, and this has been possible greatly due to our system of capitalism. Capitalism and socialism go together like light and dark or hot and cold. They cannot exist at the same time and in the same place.

Socialism is much like an expensive fishing lure. It is very attractive, colorful, and shiny at first glance, but there's a hidden hook. Many well-meaning individuals are attracted by socialism as it seeks to provide for the welfare of everyone. There is something laudable and appealing about all of us working together to provide for everyone. The only problem with socialism is the simple fact that it doesn't work.

Capitalism allows you to give everyone more without giving anyone less. Socialism requires you to give everyone less if you give anyone more.

One of the best books on the subject is Steve Forbes' *How Capitalism Will Save Us.* For over 20 years, I have been privileged to have an ongoing friendship with Steve Forbes. Whenever I am in New York City, we schedule a morning or afternoon to meet at the Forbes Building in the second-floor library established by Steve's father, Malcolm Forbes. In these meetings, Mr. Forbes and I discuss a number of world issues and political topics, but eventually the conversation moves toward the subject of money.

There's probably no one in the world today more associated with wealth, money, and capitalism than Steve Forbes. We actually filmed one of our library conversations. It was included in the special features on the menu of the DVD version of *The Lamp* movie based on one of my novels. You can enjoy a portion of that conversation in this video: www.youtube.com/watch?v=bzCWz_KHt7k.

All honorable people want to help those among us who are less fortunate. You can go into any city and look at the names on hospitals, schools, universities, parks, and other institutions that make the world a better place, and you will find they are invariably named after and were donated by capitalists. Not all rich people help the poor, but no poor people can financially help anyone.

As you go through your day today, carefully examine the rhetoric and the reality of the political discussion.

*Today's the day!*

# HEARING THE WRITTEN WORD

FOR THOUSANDS OF YEARS HUMANS HAVE SHARED THEIR thoughts, ideas, advice, and deepest secrets with one another by writing them down. Our earliest evidence of this is the many examples of picture writing left on cave walls around the world. Then humans discovered they could write on papyrus, and eventually wood was processed into paper much like what we know today between the covers of a book.

In the middle of the 15$^{th}$ century, one of the greatest and most impactful inventions the world has ever known came into being when Johann Gutenberg built a printing press. This brought the written word and all of its potential for education, socialization, and inspiration to the masses. Books that had been rare treasures, made individually by hand, were now mass produced and became commonplace for working-class people everywhere.

Gutenberg's printed books became the standard for the next five centuries until an incredible breakthrough changed the state-of-the-art. Somewhere in the mid-20$^{th}$ century, audiobooks were born. First, they were available on vinyl albums, then tapes, followed by CDs, and now audiobooks can be delivered via a simple digital download that would have seemed like a miracle to Gutenberg.

As the author, it's embarrassing to admit to you that when I could read with my eyes as you are reading these words, I don't know that I ever read a whole book cover to cover. Throughout my school days and as a young adult, reading was not a priority, so I did as little of it as possible just to get by. Then after losing my sight in my late 20s, I discovered audiobooks, and my whole world changed.

I worked with the manufacturer that developed the first variable-speed tape player, and I began consuming audiobooks at several times their normal speed. This has enabled me to read a book a day for more than 25 years. Becoming a reader enabled me to become a writer and then a columnist. I've enjoyed experiencing six of my books being made into major motion pictures with several more of my novels slated for the silver screen.

As someone who writes books I can't read that are turned into movies I can't watch, I realize that audiobooks have become my lifeline to the world; and not just our world today, but the world of William Shakespeare, F. Scott Fitzgerald, Charles Dickens, Dante, and countless others.

For obvious reasons, I insist on having all of my books released by my publisher as audiobooks in addition to the print versions. For the last several years, my audiobooks have been produced by a talented voiceover artist and recording engineer named Rich Germaine. You can check out Rich's work on my titles and others at:

http://www.betterlifeaudio.com/product-category/authors/.

There is simply no excuse for not becoming a reader. Whether you use your eyes or your ears, the world awaits.

As you go through your day today, commit to being a reader whether you choose to see it or hear it.

***Today's the day!***

# UNDERSTANDING CENTENARIANS

O NE OF MY FAVORITE AUTHORS, LOUIS L'AMOUR, WROTE, "No person can be judged except against the backdrop of the time and place in which they lived."

The fastest-growing demographic in America is made up of people who are over 100 years old. It's important for us to realize what the world looked like when they came into it.

A century ago:

- The average life expectancy for men was 47 years.

- Fuel for cars was sold in drug stores only.

- Only 14 percent of the homes had a bathtub.

- Only 8 percent of the homes had a telephone.

- The maximum speed limit in most cities was 10 mph.

- The tallest structure in the world was the Eiffel Tower.

- The average U.S. wage in 1910 was 22 cents per hour.

- The average U.S. worker made between $200 and $400 per year.

- A competent accountant could expect to earn $2,000 per year.

- A dentist $2,500 per year.

- A veterinarian between $1,500 and $4,000 per year.

- A mechanical engineer about $5,000 per year.

- More than 95 percent of all births took place at home.

- Ninety percent of all doctors had no college education. Instead, they attended so-called medical schools, many of which were condemned in the press and the government as substandard.

- Sugar cost 4 cents a pound, eggs were 14 cents a dozen, and coffee was 15 cents a pound.

- The five leading causes of death were: 1) pneumonia; 2) tuberculosis; 3) diarrhea; 4) heart disease; 5) stroke.

- The American flag had 45 stars.

- The population of Las Vegas, Nevada, was only 30.

- Crossword puzzles, canned beer, and iced tea hadn't been invented yet.

- There was neither a Mother's Day nor a Father's Day.

- Two out of every ten adults couldn't read or write, and only 6 percent of all Americans had graduated from high school.

- Marijuana, heroin, and morphine were all available over the counter at local corner drugstores. Back then, pharmacists said, "Heroin clears the complexion, gives buoyancy to the mind, regulates the stomach and bowels, and is, in fact, a perfect guardian of health!"

- There were about 230 reported murders per year in the entire USA.

Now in the 21st century, it's important for us to understand the perspective of people who lived most of their lives in the 20th century and who were raised by people who lived in the 19th century. We all view things from our own perspective, but we must remember, other people have their own perspectives.

As you go through your day today, reflect upon where the last century has brought us and where the next century will take us.

*Today's the day!*

# HAPPY HOLIDAYS

MY WEEKLY COLUMNS ARE READ BY MILLIONS OF PEOPLE around the world in diverse locations, cultures, and countries. There are a variety of customs various people utilize to celebrate the holiday season, but the majority of these customs focus on faith, friends, and family. Here in the United States where I live, we have allowed the commercialization of the holiday season to rule our lives for the last several months of each calendar year. What should be a blessed time of celebration and sharing has become a hectic season of scheduling commitments and gift exchange obligations.

One of my mentors taught me early in my career to "Remember, when everything's going wrong, go back and reflect on what you were doing when things were going right."

There was a time in our society when the holiday season reflected our values of faith, friends, and family. In the past, people gave and received fewer gifts and attended far fewer holiday events. It would seem that fewer gifts and holiday celebrations would have diminished the season, but in reality, having fewer financial and time commitments allowed past generations to focus on the true meaning of the season. We can get so caught up in the glitter, decorations, and symbols of the holidays that we overlook what really matters.

If you and your family exchanged fewer gifts, attended fewer parties, and avoided the commercial demands of the season, you would discover that you would receive more blessings from the holidays. Many great truths in this life involve a paradox, which simply means that wisdom is often counterintuitive. If we only gave one person a gift each year and only attended one holiday celebration, that single gift and celebration would take on a new meaning; but when we exchange gifts with everyone and try to attend every party, a hectic sense of obligation and chaos sets in.

In the computer world, Facebook has taught us all a great lesson. When you identify hundreds or even thousands of people as our "friends," it diminishes the experience. If you had to focus on one true friend, the experience is magnified. Frank Capra, who directed the great holiday classic movie *It's a Wonderful Life*, got the idea for the story from a greeting card that said, in part, "No person can ever be considered poor if they have one true friend."

Begin your holiday transformation this year by telling each friend and family member how much they mean to you when you give them their gift. You will discover that the gifts will simply be a token of the love you feel for that person.

As you go through your day today, remember when it comes to holidays, far less can be much more.

**Today's the day!**

# HOLIDAY HAPPINESS

EVERYONE WANTS TO HAVE HAPPINESS FOR THEMSELVES AND their loved ones around the holidays. We wish people "Merry Christmas," "Happy Holidays," and "Happy New Year," but rarely do we consider what really makes us happy during the holiday season and throughout the year. If you think back on past holiday seasons when you were particularly happy, you will likely discover it had more to do with gifts you gave, people you were with, and activities you enjoyed rather than something you received.

While it is the season for giving, if we want to make people really happy, we need to look beyond just the standard stuff we buy at the mall, wrap up, and hand to someone. We need to explore the concept of sharing an experience, giving of ourselves, or engaging in a giving activity with our loved ones.

I often ask people to share with me their favorite holiday memories. Among my favorites are people who recount the experience of going as a family to serve homeless people holiday meals, giving toys or bicycles to less fortunate children, or simply spending quality time with special friends or loved ones. I actually have a friend who received a luxury automobile with a giant bow wrapped around it, parked in the driveway, as a Christmas gift, but when I asked her to share her favorite holiday memory, it involved going through a family photo album with her great aunt.

We've often heard it said but seldom do we act upon the fact that "it is more blessed to give than to receive." In my novel *The Ultimate Gift* and the movie based on that book, a prominent theme is the gift of giving. This concept is foreign to many people because, with the rush and commercialism during the holiday season, giving can seem like more of a chore or an obligation than a gift.

We are never too busy to give a kindness, share a memory, or engage in service to others. This time of year, people seem to be worried about spending too much money and overcharging their credit cards, but giving of yourself and sharing memories remain no-cost but priceless elements in the gift of giving.

As you go through your day today, give the gifts that matter. Share your time and your love.

**Today's the day!**

# THE POETS

IGOT UP EARLY ONE MORNING AS IS MY HABIT AND TURNED ON
my satellite radio to catch the business report from Asia. I was
a bit surprised but pleased to hear Merle Haggard singing *Are
the Good Times Really Over for Good?* emanating from my speakers. My first thought was that Merle's lyrics were a lead-in to
some kind of business story dealing with an economic decline
or stock market downturn, but after they played the entire song,
a business reporter from Tokyo solemnly announced that Merle
Haggard had passed away on his 79th birthday.

Whether you like country music in general or Merle Haggard specifically, you would have to admit that Merle Haggard's
influence on several generations of musicians and songwriters
is indisputable. He will forever be known as The Poet of the
Common Man. This is a description that he modestly declined
throughout his life but will remain as his enduring legacy. For
more than half a century, Merle Haggard wrote and sang about
the trials, triumphs, and tribulations of everyday people.

Merle Haggard's parents had their roots in my home state of
Oklahoma and were among those who became known as Okies as
they migrated to California during the Dust Bowl days throughout the 1930s and 40s.

Among other things, Merle Haggard was known for his
prison songs which, to a certain extent, came out of his own

experience of being behind bars. He was pardoned by Ronald Reagan and more than paid his debt to society throughout the ensuing half century of his creative output.

Being a true poet and being connected to common people, Merle Haggard always made me think of another of my favorite poets, Rudyard Kipling. In Kipling's transformational poem *If*—in which he gives poignant and powerful advice to his son about becoming a man—the final stanza describes the life of Merle Haggard.

> *If you can talk with crowds and keep your virtue,*
> *Or walk with Kings—nor lose the common touch,*
> *If neither foes nor loving friends can hurt you,*
> *If all men count with you, but none too much;*
> *If you can fill the unforgiving minute*
> *With sixty seconds' worth of distance run,*
> *Yours is the Earth and everything that's in it,*
> *And—which is more—you'll be a Man, my son!*

Whenever great people pass away, it should give us pause to reflect upon their accomplishments and redouble our efforts regarding our own goals, destiny, and legacy. Poets like Merle Haggard, Rudyard Kipling, and others have inspired me to present my own message in poetry.

> *Hold on to your dreams and stand tall*
> *Even when those around you would force you to crawl.*
> *Hold on to your dreams as a race you must run*
> *Even when reality whispers, "You'll never be done!"*
> *Hold on to your dreams and wait for the magic to come,*
> *Because on that miraculous day, your*
> *dreams and your reality*
> *Will merge into one.*

As you go through your day today, remember the great poets and common people.

*Today's the day!*

# Changing the Calendar

E ACH YEAR AS JANUARY 1ST APPROACHES, MOST OF US ENGAGE in the time-tested ritual of getting a new calendar. I realize a lot of people use electronic devices and cell phone applications to document their upcoming activities and commitments, but nevertheless, there is that annual feeling of a fresh start and a new beginning. It puts me in mind of the first day of school with a clean notebook or a fresh tablet. The future seems pregnant with possibility.

Many people engage in the annual frustration of establishing New Year's resolutions. These rarely work because most resolutions require us to change our performance or modify our behavior. Change doesn't result from getting a new calendar or declaring a New Year's resolution. Change happens when we face the discomfort of giving up our old patterns and established routines. Most goals and resolutions go unfulfilled because people simply never buy in to the proposition that true and lasting change is possible.

Your past does not equal your future. Virtually everything in your life today is based upon choices you've made in the past. Whether it's your job, your career, your friends, your hobbies, your physical fitness, your attitude, your financial stability, or your faith, your life today is but a reflection of the choices you have made in the past.

We live in a society in which not many want to take responsibility for their current conditions, their performance, or the results they live with. Unfortunately, unless or until you and I accept the fact that we are where we are because of the choices we've made in the past, we cannot accept the promise and the possibility of tomorrow based on the choices we make today.

Either we control our lives or we don't. If we control our lives, we can change course anytime we want, including New Year's Day. If we believe we don't control our destiny, we will live out our lives as victims with our only consolation being the excuses we develop and the ability to blame others. As you contemplate the New Year, please accept the premise on which everything depends—change is possible and in your control.

As you go through your day today, take responsibility for past choices and choose greatness for your future.

*Today's the day!*

# Another New Year

WELL, HERE WE ARE AGAIN FACING ANOTHER NEW YEAR. WE have a new calendar, a clean slate, and endless possibilities. Unfortunately, the majority of us will, once again, make one of two bad mistakes that will guarantee we will be at this same place and point in life next year. Every new year, people either commit to unrealistic, unreasonable resolutions they never realize, or they commit to absolutely nothing which they continue to realize.

There is nothing magic about the new year. We can declare a new year, new decade, or a turning point in our life any time we want to, but the new year seems to offer us a clear delineation between old and new that we can use to our advantage.

Avoid resolutions—establish some life goals. Resolutions are wishes or dreams that we casually make and even more casually forget. Goals must be personal, realistic, and measurable. You can establish a New Year's resolution because your spouse thinks you should, your mother-in-law has been pressuring you, or your next-door-neighbor suggested it, but a goal must be personal. It must matter to you and you alone and be worth the price you're going to pay to reach it.

Once you have identified a personal goal, you must be sure it is realistic. If you've been watching too much late-night TV or surfing the Internet too much, you might be tempted to set a goal to lose 50 pounds by next Thursday, become a millionaire by the weekend, or meet the love of your life by lunchtime today.

Becoming successful is rarely a pioneering effort. Most goals that you and I want to achieve have been achieved by others before us. Don't ever take advice from anyone who doesn't have what you want. Before you set a goal, find someone who has achieved that same goal, and mirror their activity. This will enable you to mirror their results.

Finally, once you have established a goal that is personal and realistic, you must make sure it's measurable. You might set a goal to establish peace on earth and good will toward men or have a better relationship with your spouse and kids, or be a better employee, but you'll never realize any of these objectives until you quantify them in a way that is measurable. The thing you can measure is the thing you can move. I hope you will abandon the new year's resolution trap in favor of the life-goal path. If so, I will truly wish you a Happy New Year.

As you go through your day today, make sure your goals are personal, realistic, and measurable.

*Today's the day!*

# STATE OF MIND

I LIVE IN THE UNITED STATES, AND ONE OF THE GREAT THINGS about the U.S. is that we have 50 separate and distinct states. There is something special, fun, and unique reported about each of them.

Alabama: The first state to have 9-1-1 started in 1968.

Alaska: Alaska's name is based on the Eskimo word Alakshak meaning great lands or peninsula.

Arizona: Is the only state in the continental U.S. that does not follow Daylight Savings Time.

Arkansas: Has the only active diamond mine in the U.S.

California: Its economy is so large that if it were a country, it would rank eighth in the entire world.

Colorado: In 1976, it became the only state to turn down the Olympics.

Connecticut: The Frisbee was invented here at Yale University.

Delaware: Sixth most densely populated state.

Florida: At 874.3 square miles, Jacksonville is the largest city in the U.S.

Georgia: It was here, in 1886, that pharmacist John Pemberton made the first vat of Coca-Cola.

Hawaii: NASA astronauts from Apollo missions 13 to 17 were trained for moon voyages by walking on its lava fields.

Idaho: Idaho's capitol building is the only one in the United States heated by geothermal water. The hot water is tapped and pumped from a source 3,000 feet underground.

Illinois: Des Plaines is home to the first McDonalds.

Indiana: Home to Santa Claus, Indiana, where a nonprofit organization answers thousands of children's letters to Santa each year.

Iowa: Fenelon Place Elevator in Dubuque is the world's steepest and shortest scenic railway.

Kansas: Liberal, Kansas, has an exact replica of the house in *The Wizard of Oz.*

Kentucky: The song *Happy Birthday to You* was the creation of two Louisville sisters in 1893 but was originally titled *Good Morning to All.*

Louisiana: Has parishes instead of counties because it was originally Spanish and French territory divided by church boundaries.

Maine: Has 3,166 offshore islands. Only about 1,200 Maine coast islands have an acre or more, and 600 comprise 95 percent of the island acreage.

Maryland: The state sport is jousting, a competition between two armored contestants mounted on horses in which each tries to strike the other with a lance.

Massachusetts: The Fig Newton is named after Newton, Massachusetts.

Michigan: Fremont, home to Gerber, is the baby food capital of the world.

Minnesota: Inventions include masking and Scotch tape, Wheaties cereal, and the Bundt pan.

Mississippi: In 1902 while on a hunting expedition in Sharkey County, President Theodore (Teddy) Roosevelt refused to shoot a captured bear. This act resulted in the creation of the world-famous teddy bear.

Missouri: Is the birthplace of the ice cream cone.

Montana: A sapphire from Montana is in the Crown Jewels of England.

Nebraska: The largest porch swing in the world is located in Hebron and can sit 25 adults.

Nevada: Has more mountain ranges than any other U.S. state.

New Hampshire: The first free public library was established in Peterborough in 1833.

New Jersey: Has the most diners in the world and is sometimes referred to as The Diner Capitol of the World.

New Mexico: Las Cruces makes the world's largest enchilada (about 10.5 feet in diameter) the first weekend in October at the Whole Enchilada Fiesta.

New York: It is home to the nation's oldest cattle ranch started in 1747 in Montauk.

North Carolina: Home of the first Krispy Kreme doughnut.

North Dakota: Rigby, North Dakota, is the exact geographic center of North America.

Ohio: The first professional baseball team was born in Cincinnati in 1869—the Cincinnati Red Stockings.

Oklahoma: The grounds of the state capitol are covered by operating oil wells.

Oregon: Crater Lake is the deepest in the U.S. and was actually pooled in the remains of a volcano.

Pennsylvania: The first daily newspaper was published in Philadelphia on September 21, 1784.

Rhode Island: The nation's oldest bar, the White Horse Tavern, opened here in 1673.

South Carolina: The first organized game of golf played in the U.S. took place in Charleston.

South Dakota: Belle Fourche is the geographical center of the United States (including Alaska and Hawaii), designated in 1959 and noted by an official marker and sheepherder's monument called a *Stone Johnnie.*

Tennessee: Nashville's Grand Ole Opry is the longest-running live radio show in the world.

Texas: Dr. Pepper was invented in Waco and first served around 1885.

Utah: The first Kentucky Fried Chicken franchise restaurant opened here in 1952.

Vermont: The first state admitted to the Union after the ratification of the Constitution.

Virginia: The states of Kentucky and West Virginia were formed from sections of the state of Virginia.

Washington: The popular game Pictionary was invented here.

West Virginia: Mother's Day was first observed at Andrews Church in Grafton on May 10, 1908.

Wisconsin: The only state to offer a Master Cheesemaker program. It takes three years to complete, and you need ten years of cheese making experience before you can even apply as a candidate.

Wyoming: The first state to give women the right to vote in 1869.

As you go through your day today, explore all the treasures in your state.

**Today's the day!**

# FINANCIAL FINESSE

# BILLION-DOLLAR BLIND SPOT

UNLESS YOU ARE JUST RETURNING FROM A PROLONGED SPACE voyage or have been living in a remote cave somewhere, you are no doubt aware of when the Powerball lottery jackpot exceeds $1 billion. A billion dollars is certainly newsworthy and grabs our attention, but let's try to get a bit of perspective.

Please understand that I certainly don't object—for people who can afford it—to anyone buying a lottery ticket. In fact, I don't object to anyone buying anything if they can afford it. If you are spending your hard-earned cash on something you really want to have, and if you've prudently taken care of all your debts, expenses, and emergency-fund contingencies, you won't find me objecting to anything you want to buy.

Benjamin Franklin is known for saying, "A penny saved is a penny earned." Mr. Franklin's wisdom enlightens us that any money we don't spend today is like new money we just earned that we can spend tomorrow. I consider myself to be a student of Benjamin Franklin's as he seemed to have more wisdom to share on a broader spectrum of topics than almost anyone in history. If old Ben were alive today and saw the extreme amounts of debt carried by most people in the 21$^{st}$ century, I believe he might say of people in debt, "A penny spent is a penny borrowed."

It's important to put all of your spending in perspective. If you are carrying a credit card balance or have consumer debt of any type, you must consider any amount you spend as an amount borrowed. This logic is valid because if you didn't spend the money on lottery tickets or any other frivolous expenditure, you would be able to pay that money down on your debt; therefore, spending money on anything that is not a necessity while you are in debt is the same as borrowing the money.

National statistics show us that the average long-term lottery player buys several hundred dollars' worth of tickets each month. Most of these lottery players would be ecstatic if they won a million-dollar jackpot just once in their lives. Ironically, if they had simply put $40 a week into a stock index fund throughout their working lives, they would be millionaires. These projections are based on historical returns that would have been valid any time in the last half century.

Never trade a sure thing for pie in the sky, especially if you have to borrow the money to do it.

As you go through your day today, put money in the proper perspective. Then you can afford anything, but not everything.

*Today's the day!*

# THE MONEY SHORTAGE MYTH

EXPERTS TELL US THAT THE NUMBER ONE CAUSE OF DIVORCE, domestic abuse, suicide, and stress in our society today stems from money shortages. As a blind person myself who started my business and financial life with less than nothing, I understand this dynamic; however, as a long-term chronic condition, I do not believe in the concept of a money shortage. Money is not a cause. It's a result.

If the electricity is cut off at your house, you might instantly believe you have a light shortage, but in reality, the light is the result and the electricity or lack thereof is the cause. Many people who believe they are the victims of a money shortage would be shocked to discover they are predominantly the cause of the money shortage. While I don't believe people have money shortages, I do believe they experience shortages of ideas, motivation, persistence, creativity, and vision.

As someone who has worked in the financial services and financial planning industries for over a quarter of a century, I have met many people who were broke when they graduated from college and began their careers. It is not unusual to experience a tight budget when you are first starting out; but ironically, the majority of these people are experiencing a lifetime money shortage even though today many of them are earning six-figure incomes and beyond. We can always outspend our income and create a money shortage. One need look no further than the United States federal government to see this phenomenon in action.

Most of the problems that individuals, couples, and families suffer through that are labeled as a money shortage could have been avoided with a few hundred or a few thousand dollars. As a multimillionaire today, I certainly can vividly remember when the lack of a few hundred or a few thousand dollars created a crisis in my life, but I see so many people today who can't afford to replace the worn-out tires on their BMW, Lexus, or Mercedes. I was shocked to learn in a recent national study that most significant home repairs on million-dollar houses have to be financed.

We create money shortages in the same way that the federal government does. We spend all we have and all we can borrow. Using this formula, you can double your income today or multiply it by ten, and in a very short period of time, you will be experiencing a money shortage.

The positive side of realizing that we are our own worst enemy financially is that we come to understand that we are in control. Taking control is the first step to solving any problem. The next time you feel like you and your family are experiencing a *money* shortage, examine the numbers closely, and you will likely discover you have a *control* shortage.

As you go through your day today, control your money before it takes control of you.

*Today's the day!*

# POSITIONS AND PERSPECTIVES

FOR MORE THAN A DECADE, I HAVE BEEN PART OF A HEDGE fund. It is a private equity investment group made up of several dozen entrepreneurs and investors. I am among the youngest members of the group, and I have profited not only from the collective investment advice but from the wisdom and experience of the other members as well.

When we evaluate someone's opinion, we must calibrate their perspective before we act upon it. After our private investment group evaluated a certain startup entrepreneurial venture, we discussed our thoughts. Seated on my right was a self-made millionaire with more than 50 years of experience as an investor. He gave his opinion on the deal we were evaluating by saying, "We probably wouldn't lose all our money in a deal like that." Seated on my left was an enthusiastic, hard-driving business owner I really respect. He said, "We should all mortgage everything we own, and go into this deal with both feet."

An outside observer might assume the colleague sitting on my right was negative or lukewarm on the investment while the colleague on my left was over-the-moon in his positive feelings for the proposal. In reality, as I sat there listening to the feedback from two people I respect, I mentally graded them both as a 6 on a scale of one to ten. They each have a perspective that causes them to evaluate opportunities from very different perspectives.

My weekly columns are read by many people from all around the world, but in the United States, we have a government that is intended to be of the people, by the people, and for the people. Researchers from Johns Hopkins University studied the views and perspectives of government employees who work inside the Beltway in Washington, DC. Their research revealed that many of the individuals who are employed to serve the public have a very low opinion of voters and the general population.

The research summary states, "Government workers generally feel that the public is uninformed, knows very little about key issues, and holds opinions that can be ignored." The study showed that Washington insiders are wealthier, whiter, and more educated than the average citizen. Seventy-three percent of government officials believe that the public knows little or nothing about how to help the poor. Seventy-one percent of our government employees believe the public knows little or nothing about science or technology. Sixty-one percent of our public servants were revealed to believe that the average American knows almost nothing about childcare.

The researchers concluded that since these government officials believe that the general public knows little or nothing about pertinent issues, that government officials should make decisions themselves regardless of public opinion.

The Beltway perspective can be further understood when you realize that 91 percent of people who work for federal agencies are white, compared to 78 percent of the general population; federal employees earn 48 percent more than workers in the private sector; and 60 percent of government employees who work in Washington, DC, are Democrats as opposed to 35 percent in the general public. This may explain why Americans are often perplexed by policies that come out of Washington, DC.

As you go through your day today, evaluate someone's perspective before you evaluate their opinion.

*Today's the day!*

# THEY DIDN'T LEARN

W E'VE ALL HEARD THAT EXPERIENCE IS THE BEST TEACHER; therefore, the longer we live, the more we should know. Unfortunately, some recent statistics indicate that the Baby Boomers did not learn from the Greatest Generation. Baby Boomers, individuals born between 1946 and 1964, were raised by parents and influenced by others who lived through the Great Depression and World War II.

The Great Depression and World War II offered many lessons dealing with saving and sacrifice. Great fortunes are historically built during some of the most difficult economic times. Baby Boomers who saw the aftermath of this pivotal, historical period and were influenced by parents, teachers, and others who lived through it have too often failed to put those historical lessons into practice.

2016 statistics reveal:

- Fifty-nine percent of Baby Boomers are relying significantly or totally on social security for retirement income. This is up from 43 percent in 2014. The stability of the Social Security program is debatable, but cuts of up to 20 percent in real benefit income may become a reality in the coming years.

- Forty-five percent of Baby Boomers facing retirement have absolutely no savings to support or supplement their golden years. This alarming number is up from 20 percent in 2014 who had no retirement nest egg.

- Over 30 percent of Baby Boomers are continuing to work beyond the point they had anticipated retiring. Over a quarter of Baby Boomers say they will not be able to retire until after age 70. Contrast this with only 17 percent of Boomers anticipated retiring after 70 just five years ago.

- Thirty percent of Baby Boomers report they have stopped contributing to their retirement fund, and 16 percent have actually depleted their retirement savings by taking an early withdrawal. Only two years ago, 80 percent of Baby Boomers reported contributing consistently to their retirement.

- Forty-four percent of Baby Boomers reach retirement age with significant debt loads. The percentage of retired people with debt a generation ago was only 30 percent.

If the Baby Boomers haven't learned from history, hopefully the rest of us can learn from the Baby Boomers.

Our grandparents could depend on pensions and defined benefit plans that guaranteed their retirement. You and I have the privilege of raising the bar and establishing our own retirement level, which is a huge advantage, but only if we proceed with diligence and consistency as we move toward retirement.

As you go through your day today, learn from the Baby Boomers, and plan for your future.

*Today's the day!*

# LAND OF THE FREE

I AM VERY PROUD, PLEASED, AND BLESSED TO BE AN AMERICAN. My weekly columns are read by people literally all around the world. I have been contacted by *Winners' Wisdom* column readers who live in dozens of different countries. On several occasions, I have been contacted by readers who are citizens of countries that I was not familiar with and was, therefore, compelled to sharpen my geography knowledge.

Opportunities abound here in America. No matter what you may hear in the media, it is easier and simpler to become wealthy in the United States today than ever before. Tax advantages and investment strategies exist that allow everyone with a little bit of discipline and diligence to become financially independent.

Throughout my travels across the country and around the world over a number of years, I have conducted my own informal research into immigrants' work ethic and financial success. My curiosity began when I met a Somalian immigrant who was driving me from the airport in San Diego to the resort where I was speaking. He and I struck up a conversation and became friends. Over the past 18 years, I have made more than 40 trips to San Diego for speeches on the same resort island, and my Somalian friend has been my driver on every occasion.

When I first met him, he had just arrived in our country and was working diligently to save enough money to bring his family from Somalia to America. After several years, he reached his goal but continued to pursue his own version of the American dream. Today, I'm pleased to report that my Somalian friend who will shortly become an American citizen owns a fleet of limousines, a gas station, a convenience store, and equity in several other businesses throughout southern California.

When he arrived in the United States, my friend did not know our language, our culture, or our business environment. Today, he speaks fluent, if heavily accented, English; engages in the best of our culture while still having a passion for his African heritage; and has become an astute and shrewd American businessman. If you were to judge my friend's path to success from the streets of Somalia to the lifestyle he enjoys today, you would realize that any high school graduate in the United States is more than halfway up the mountain my friend has climbed. He spent over a decade just getting to the starting blocks where most of us begin our careers; but nevertheless, he has become the envy of many Americans who are convinced that my friend is lucky or found some secret to success.

His success secret is the same one you and I can utilize. Believe in the American dream, and work hard.

As you go through your day today, remember 95 percent of the people on earth would give everything to be where you are.

*Today's the day!*

# THE ART OF PRODUCTIVITY

PRODUCTIVITY, OR BEING PRODUCTIVE, IS NOTHING MORE than making maximum efficient progress toward our goals. If we have established appropriate personal and professional goals, there's nothing more important than being productive.

A number of years ago, I combined forces with Steve Forbes and legendary coach John Wooden to produce a book and training program based on productivity. This material has been refined and updated and was released in 2017 titled *The Art of Productivity* with a Foreword by Steve Forbes. (Visit www.JimStovallBooks.com.)

Before you can focus on productivity, you must have specific, meaningful, realistic, and achievable goals. If we are traveling along a highway, we might assume that the car that is moving the fastest is the most productive; however, unless we know where people are trying to go, we can't measure their productivity solely based on their speed. One motorist might be unsafely driving well above the speed limit endangering the person's life, the lives of their passengers, and other motorists. The driver of another vehicle may be intending to reach a destination to the north as they rapidly drive south, which is actually counterproductive.

Once we have established appropriate goals, productivity can be broken down into three components—motivation, communication, and implementation.

Motivation is the drive and determination that makes us get up every morning, leave our comfortable home, and pursue our passion. If you are pursuing anything other than your passion, it will be impossible to consistently stay motivated. In my work as an entrepreneur, executive, and consultant, I have dealt with countless people around the world who have achieved a high level of productivity because they are motivated. They may all be equally motivated, but they are invariably motivated by different factors. Some people are motivated by money, others by titles, some by inclusion, others by recognition, and still other people are motivated by internal factors known only to them.

You must find your own individual motivation, or you can't be productive and achieve success. If you are not totally motivated, it is inevitable that you will be competing in the marketplace against individuals and organizations that are motivated. Most sporting events prove the point that the race rarely goes to the strongest or swiftest, but instead, the winners in sports and in life are those who become the most motivated and the most productive.

The second element of productivity is communication. No one succeeds by themselves. We all have a team, and in order to be productive, you must be motivated and then communicate your motivation to the entire team. As in motivation, there are a myriad of communication styles. Some people prefer to be told. Others need to see it in writing. Some people need to repeat it back or experience an example of the concept being communicated. There's no right or wrong way to communicate with your team, but you must determine what works best for those around you and communicate in the way that they can best receive your message.

Once you have established motivation and created communication, you must implement. In our world today, when it's all said and done, there's a lot said and very little done. Some people implement best on their own, others need to work as part of a team, some people are most productive working in a linear fashion, while others prefer to multitask. Whatever the case may be with you and your team, you simply need to finetune your productivity, and you can change your life, your organization, and the world.

As you go through your day today, remember to focus on motivation, communication, and implementation.

*Today's the day!*

# ALREADY 59

MY 59TH BIRTHDAY WAS SIGNIFICANT TO ME BECAUSE I BEGAN my career as an investment broker and still write and speak about financial success. Age 59 is a critical point in personal financial planning because within the year you turn 59½, you can begin withdrawing money from your IRA or 401K without a penalty.

I remember as a young man when I first started explaining to people that they couldn't take any of their retirement funds until they were 59½, it sounded like forever to me, but as most of us are discovering, time does fly and before you know it, you have reached an age you could not have imagined when you were a teenager or young adult.

I have had great financial success in my businesses and through my books and movies. I outline this in detail in my book *The Millionaire Map*; however, today I feel that one of my most significant financial successes has come from becoming a millionaire in what I think of as the ordinary way.

A little over 20 years ago, I began investing in an IRA, and then when my company began offering a 401K, I participated at the same level any employee or business owner can. Today, I am pleased that these funds have built up to millionaire status. This means that anyone who works diligently, saves regularly, and invests persistently can become a millionaire if they start early and stay with it.

The fastest-growing group of millionaires in America are not entrepreneurs or corporate CEOs. They are, instead, retirement-fund millionaires who invested in tax-deferred or tax-advantaged accounts that are available to all of us. Most of us wish we had started saving and investing earlier, but that ship has already sailed. The opportunity we have before us now is to get started today and invest regularly.

I highly recommend that you invest through a payroll deduction at work or through an automatic withdrawal in your own self-directed account. In this way, your monthly contributions to your financial future are made automatically and take no thought or real discipline on your part. You will have to make a decision to stop investing instead of being forced to make a decision every month whether-or-not to stay the course.

Whether you have already passed the trigger age of 59½, or whether you are just getting started and retirement seems a million miles away, I can assure you the future will be here sooner than you think. While none of us can stop the inevitable march of time, we can make sure that our golden years will be everything we want them to be financially.

As you go through your day today, invest early, consistently, and persistently.

*Today's the day!*

# THE FRIENDLY SKIES

IN 2017, THERE WAS AN INCIDENT ON A UNITED AIRLINES flight that has now received worldwide attention. A ticketed passenger who was already in his assigned seat was forcibly removed from the plane and was injured in the process. This brings up several critical issues surrounding policy, publicity, and public relations.

Everyone who is in business or works for a business should be concerned about these types of incidents. Not only was a paying customer injured, but millions of dollars' worth of reputation and goodwill were instantly lost.

There was a time when such an incident would have been controlled by corporate officials or the media as they had access to the information pipeline; but today, another passenger with a cell phone changed the dynamic and demonstrated to us all the power of publicity.

All businesses have regrettable occurrences. It is simply a matter of how they handle them that spells the difference between success and failure. A number of years ago, through no fault of their own, Tylenol had a corporate crisis when an unknown individual tampered with some of their product that was already on the shelf. Instead of denying, delaying, or evading the issue, Tylenol got out in front of it and turned a short-term crisis into a long-term, reputation-building opportunity. They pulled all the product from the shelves and replaced it with a new tamper-proof product. While this was obviously expensive, time consuming, and labor intensive, it paid off for Tylenol in the long run. Had they not managed the crisis, the name Tylenol would be a distant memory in a long-forgotten business textbook.

Overbooking seats on airlines is currently a legal and acceptable practice that should probably be reviewed; however, on the flight in question, United Airlines offered passengers an incentive to reticket, but no one accepted the offer. I have no doubt if they had increased the offer by a few hundred dollars, eventually they would have gotten one of the passengers to volunteer to be reticketed on another flight, and the whole matter would have been resolved. Now, United Airlines is facing potential lawsuits, bad publicity, and loss of corporate reputation that represents literally millions of dollars.

In a perfect world, we should treat one another as we would like to be treated because it is the fundamental element of all successful human encounters, but failing that, the Golden Rule simply makes good business sense.

I am certain there were many passengers on that flight and countless more around the world who saw the video who were greatly stressed and have determined to never fly United Airlines again. Many of them may have reached for a Tylenol to ease their tension and ensuing headache.

As you go through your day today, remember the value of a good reputation and how quickly it can be lost.

***Today's the day!***

# STATISTICS, TRENDS, AND OTHER MYTHS

RECENTLY, I HEARD A POLITICIAN ADMONISH HIS OPPONENT in a debate by saying, "You may be entitled to your own opinion, but you're not entitled to your own facts." In reality, it seems that every person representing every side of every issue is armed with their own facts that support their position. Many times, these people do not objectively look at statistics. They instead search for statistics that support their previously held view.

Harry Truman was fond of saying, "There are lies, damned lies, and statistics." Among my entrepreneurial endeavors is a television network I founded, the Narrative Television Network. In the TV industry, we survive on ratings as these statistics determine what can be charged for commercials. Unfortunately, the statistics and ratings that were designed to clarify the marketplace are used to make it murky and even harder to understand.

If you believe the rhetoric and hyperbole, every network is number one. We have hundreds of channels available to us, and they can all find some minute spectrum of the marketplace where they come out on top. It may be overnight ratings among left-handed Eskimos, but everybody in the television industry is number one.

People often use trends and current conditions interchangeably. Current conditions might include the temperature at noon today. This can be accurately compared to last week, last month, or last year, and certain conclusions can be drawn such as it is hotter in the summer than in the winter; however, if you take a current trend and try to make it an ongoing condition, you will quickly find your argument to be absurd, irrelevant, or even dangerous.

If my beloved St. Louis Cardinals win the game on the opening day of the baseball season, which they thankfully did, this does not mean that they have established a reliable trend that will result in them winning all 162 games this season. If your child has a growth spurt and adds four inches to their height in one year, it doesn't mean this will continue and they will be 12 feet tall when they go off to college.

Warren Buffett, who often brings wisdom and clarity to complex situations, admonished over-exuberant investors by saying, "Trees don't grow to the sky." Mr. Buffett was cautioning novice investors to remember that a 20 percent stock market rise in one year makes it more likely that the following year will bring a reversal—not a continuation of the unsustainable growth rate.

As you go through your day today, remember statistics make great tools and horrible masters.

*Today's the day!*

# RAINY-DAY UMBRELLA

IN THE ANNUAL SURVEY OF AMERICAN'S SAVINGS RATES, AN alarming trend is emerging. Reports show that 60 percent of American households could not cover a $500 car repair from savings. This, reportedly, would force them to increase their credit card balance, borrow from family and friends, not pay one of their other bills, or do without a necessity in their monthly expenses.

I have been more impoverished than most people, and I'm grateful to say today I enjoy a level of wealth that exceeds all but a handful of my readers. This gives me a perspective that many people don't have.

In the process of going from overwhelming debt to building significant assets and security, there are a number of meaningful milestones. I remember paying off all of my credit card debt and committing to never carrying a balance again. I remember buying a used car and, eventually, a new car and paying cash for them. I remember paying off the mortgage on my home, and I remember writing the biggest check I have ever written in my life and giving it to charity. All of these milestones are significant to me as I look at my financial life, but they pale in comparison to the feeling of having a fully-funded rainy-day or emergency account.

It is frightening to comprehend that the majority of Americans would be thrown into financial turmoil over a $500 car repair. Most of these individuals are not poor people, they are poor managers. Prudence dictates that we have insurance to cover medical emergencies or damage to our home or car, but we must also have funds to handle or self-insure the ongoing expenses of life.

If you've owned and operated an automobile for any length of time, you realize it's not a question of *if* but *when* you will be forced to deal with a car repair. Five-hundred-dollar car repairs are not unusual. In fact, they are inevitable.

Our busy lives are filled with unanticipated expenses whether it's uninsured medical and dental procedures, appliances that need to be replaced or repaired, costs surrounding kids and school fees, or any number of financial bumps in the road, being able to cover these costs from a pre-established rainy-day or emergency fund is one of the greatest feelings you will ever enjoy. If you want to improve your financial life as well as your mental health and family dynamic, stop playing financial Russian roulette with expenses that you know are eventually headed your way.

As you go through your day today, establish a rainy-day fund that will keep you and your family safe and dry.

*Today's the day!*

# AN EDUCATION ABOUT COLLEGE

THERE IS ANOTHER FINANCIAL CRISIS LOOMING IN OUR economy. It's not a credit card crisis or another mortgage meltdown. The devastating crisis on the horizon is the looming tsunami of student loan debt. Statistics reveal that 27 percent of Americans reach retirement age still owing on student loans.

Tim Maurer is one of the great minds in the personal finance field today. I have previously co-authored two books with Tim, *Financial Crossroads* and *The Ultimate Financial Plan*. Tim's book, *Simple Money*, deals with a myriad of financial topics including how to fund a higher education while building a bright financial future.

I'm a firm believer in the value of a great education, but as Warren Buffett said, "People know the cost of everything and the value of nothing." With rare exceptions, when you look at college costs, higher prices do not always indicate greater value. In the vast research that was the basis for the bestselling book *The Millionaire Next Door*, it was revealed that a college diploma does have value in the marketplace and can be a good investment throughout a lifetime of work; however, higher tuition did not result in greater wealth.

Unless an individual is heading to law school, medical school, or a similar profession, it makes little difference where someone receives a bachelor's degree. In many areas, there are no-cost or low-cost junior colleges or community colleges whose credits transfer directly into a state university. If you pursue this course within the state where you are a resident, you may discover that you can graduate with a four-year degree and have little or no student loan debt, particularly if you are willing to work during the summers and throughout the school year.

While some college students may feel that working while attending classes and studying may hurt their academic performance, statistics show that working up to 25 hours a week can actually result in a better grade point average. I believe that the discipline required to balance work and study can produce a better student.

Student loan debt is dangerous as it is very easy to acquire and very difficult to pay off. Young people who couldn't otherwise qualify to rent an inexpensive apartment or buy a used car can instantly obligate themselves to tens of thousands of dollars in student loan debt. In most cases, student loans, along with tax obligations, are among the only debts that cannot be discharged in a bankruptcy. It's also important to remember that student loans remain whether you complete college and get a degree or not.

For these reasons, taking on student loan debt should be thought of like getting a tattoo. It may seem like a good idea at the time, but it will be with you into the future and can prove difficult, painful, and nearly impossible to get rid of.

As you go through your day today, learn the rules about getting a college education before you start.

*Today's the day!*

# LIVE LONG, LIVE WELL

THE FASTEST-GROWING DEMOGRAPHIC IN OUR SOCIETY IS made up of people who are over 100 years of age. Whether you make it to the century mark or not, it is likely that you will live longer than previous generations of your family. Living a longer life presents many exciting opportunities and a few challenges.

When our Social Security system was set up in the United States, the average recipient lived approximately one year after they retired. Now retirees routinely live several decades beyond their retirement. Determining how and when to file for your Social Security retirement benefits is one of the biggest financial decisions you will make in your life. Most people are unaware that there are many different ways you can begin receiving Social Security, and selecting the most advantageous option can result in you receiving as much as a quarter of a million dollars more throughout your retirement.

As you approach the age when you're beginning to contemplate retiring, I highly recommend you seek the advice of a fee-based financial planner who utilizes one of the up-to-date computer programs that can help you make the right decisions regarding Social Security. Information remains the most valuable commodity in the world, and for a few hundred dollars, you can get the unbiased advice of a seasoned professional. I recommend a fee-based planner for this Social Security retirement decision as they have no vested interest with respect to sales commission or other costs beyond helping you to chart the wisest course.

Financial analysts constantly debate the issue, but I believe an individual planning a long and active retirement needs a minimum of 12 times their working income as a nest egg in order to retire comfortably.

In addition to the financial matters, you can employ several strategies that may greatly impact the quantity and quality of your retirement years. Here in the 21$^{st}$ century we can control our health risks to a much greater extent than our parents or grandparents could. If you can avoid tobacco, wear your seatbelt, consume alcohol moderately, and get some regular exercise, you can greatly improve your odds of joining the centenarians' club.

Mental health professionals and physicians agree that staying physically and mentally active in retirement is a key to living long and well. Workers who transition the best into retirement are those who find a hobby or area of community service to become involved in before they actually pull the retirement trigger. The "use it or lose it" principle is a major factor in how long and how well we will likely enjoy our retirement.

As you go through your day today, plan to live long and prosper.

*Today's the day!*

# Rules, Law, and Order

Laws and rules are generally designed to keep and maintain order. While the original intent of most laws and rules are good, unfortunately, they often create a number of unintended consequences and sometimes result in chaos greater than what the rules or laws were meant to remedy.

In a perfect world, dealing with reasonable people, we would need very few laws or rules. Everyone would simply do unto others as they would like done unto them, and most laws would not be necessary. In that perfect world, rules would exist simply to document the agreed-upon policies for everyone such as which side of the street to drive on, red means stop, green means go, and other such standards.

There are relatively few among us who could not function well in the imaginary perfect world I described. Only a small number within any population sets out to intentionally break rules or ignore laws; therefore, it is important to make sure that the laws and rules that are established don't cripple the many while attempting to control the few.

In doing some research, I ran across this quote that makes the point quite eloquently. "Someone has kidnapped justice and hidden it within the law."

As a small businessperson and entrepreneur, my goal is to come to work each day, first to serve my customers and clients and second to create opportunity and a productive environment for those who work with me. Ideally, this would be a perfect formula for success for anyone in business; however, there is an ever-growing myriad of rules, regulations, and laws that confront everyone who attempts to start and run a business.

While I'm sure the original intent of most of these rules, regulations, and laws was good, the result is that the combined cost in time and money to adhere to all of the regulations cripples and destroys many fledgling businesses. Small business is the key to all financial growth and job creation; however, there are times it feels as if those we have elected to protect and serve us are out to damage or destroy us. Some of the regulations may be of limited benefit in a handful of cases, but others are simply absurd.

For many years, my company has done business with the federal government via a number of renewable, ongoing contracts. Each of these contracts requires a mountain of paperwork, most of which is nonsense, and some of it is ridiculous. For years, we were forced to fill out and sign six original copies of a document confirming that we would adhere to the "Paper Reduction Act." Beyond the insanity of creating six paper documents to confirm compliance with an act designed to reduce the use of paper, repeated inquiries over many years about the "Paper Reduction Act" revealed that no one seems to know what this regulation is or who enforces it. So at the end of a lot of wasted time and money, we have a pile of paper being generated, shipped across the country, and perpetually stored that serves no one.

When rules or laws are being established, care needs to be taken to make sure the cure is not worse than the disease.

As you go through your day today, follow all the rules as you try to eliminate the bad ones.

*Today's the day!*

# ROLE MODELING

# JOE AND LARRY

THERE ARE SEVERAL QUESTIONS WE CAN ASK OURSELVES TO perform a sort of self-examination to determine how mature, well-adjusted, and enlightened we are. One of these questions is: Am I happy when my relatives, friends, or colleagues succeed? Almost all of us would agree that we don't want our acquaintances or loved ones to fail, but the question remains, do we want them to experience success far beyond our own? This question reveals whether we believe the universe to be infinite or finite, meaning that someone else's success could limit our own possibilities.

Most of us played ball of one sort or another when we were kids. Everyone wanted to be the best ballplayer on the block. I just read a fascinating book about a man named Joe who was such a great ballplayer that he was drafted into Major League Baseball when he was just 16. But Joe wasn't even the best ballplayer who lived on his block. It turned out that Larry was the best ballplayer on the block, and they both played the same position. Joe and Larry were catchers, so even though Joe made it to the Major Leagues, Larry was even more successful in the Big Leagues and was enshrined in the Hall of Fame.

After their playing careers, Joe and Larry both pursued sports broadcasting. Larry found some success doing color commentary on Major League broadcasts, but Joe made it big with a national network and was later honored for his broadcasting prowess in the Baseball Hall of Fame.

Throughout their lives, Joe and Larry were inevitably compared to one another. When Joe was asked how it felt to be a Big League catcher after never being recognized as the best catcher in his neighborhood, he told how proud he was of Larry and how lucky he was to have Larry as a friend. After he retired as a player and began broadcasting, Larry was asked how it felt to be a Hall of Fame player on the field but then have his friend Joe eclipse his success as a broadcaster. Larry spoke fondly of Joe and how proud he was of Joe's great success as a broadcaster.

You and I can learn a lot from Joe Garagiola and Lawrence "Yogi" Berra. They were both great successes in their professional and personal lives. They realized that their own success should not be compared to anything other than their own potential. They both knew the satisfaction that comes from doing your best and succeeding while enjoying the greater success of a friend.

Joe Garagiola became famous for broadcasting sports as well as being the host of the *Today Show*. Beyond becoming a Hall of Fame baseball player, Yogi Berra became famous for a number of his offbeat sayings that carried a deeper seed of truth, but we would miss the bigger story of Joe and Larry if we didn't understand how their combined success positively impacted them both.

As you go through your day today, strive for your own success, and celebrate the success of others.

*Today's the day!*

# Meet Benjamin Franklin

B ENJAMIN FRANKLIN MAY BE BEST KNOWN TODAY FOR BEING pictured on the $100 bill. Derivatives of his name are the vernacular for that denomination of currency. While everyone would like to have another $100 bill, Ben Franklin offers us a lot more than that.

He was known as a "universal person." This denotes someone who has achieved a high level of success and expertise in many areas. In addition to being a statesman and one of the founders of the United States, Franklin was an inventor, businessman, writer, publisher, diplomat, philosopher, and much more. He had a very long, vigorous, and productive life.

He was fond of saying, "Most people die at 25 and are buried at 75." I believe we remain youthful and vigorous as long as we believe and act as if our best days are ahead. I have known many people well into their 90s such as Paul Harvey, Art Linkletter, and Coach John Wooden who were still seeking new horizons and emerging challenges. As they approached a century of life, they weren't just reflecting on their past success. They were striving for new achievements.

Benjamin Franklin was not only a big-picture visionary, but he was a meticulously detail-oriented professional. He was fond of repeating the old military wisdom, "For want of a nail, the shoe was lost. For want of a shoe, the horse was lost. For want of a horse, the rider was lost. For want of a rider, the battle was lost. For want of a battle, the war was lost. For want of the war, the kingdom was lost. All for the want of a nail."

This type of thinking made it possible for Benjamin Franklin to visualize break-through inventions and technologies while maintaining the focus and attention to detail needed to make them a reality.

I read many biographies of people I admire, and I'm always intrigued by the success people achieve that they are not primarily known for. Arnold Palmer, the championship golfer, was a pioneer in private and corporate aviation. Ted Williams, the All-Star baseball player, was a champion fly fisherman. The great comedian Red Skelton produced more acclaim and financial success with his paintings than his comedy. The skills it takes to be successful in one arena don't always apply to another, but the success principles are universal and can bring you everything you want in any field of endeavor.

The next time you reach for your wallet, think of old Ben Franklin, and consider the world of possibilities.

As you go through your day today, remember the words, life, and legacy of Benjamin Franklin.

*Today's the day!*

# How You Say It

*H*OW YOU SAY SOMETHING CAN BE AS IMPORTANT OR EVEN more important than *what* you say. Tone, inflection, and verbiage can carry the day or cost you everything. For example, in the midst of heated arguments, an explosive exchange or vindictive response might grab immediate attention, but oftentimes can cost you respect and cooperation you may need to reach your goal.

My late, great friend and mentor Coach John Wooden told me that when he was only five or six years old, he and his older brother were cleaning out the barn on their family farm. His brother teased him as older brothers will often do to younger brothers, and the young Coach Wooden responded with profanity he had heard but wasn't even sure what it meant just as his father walked into the barn. Coach Wooden told me that his father responded with love and respect asking both of the boys to promise to never use bad language again.

As Coach Wooden was telling me this story, he was 98 years of age, having lived an active and productive life until a few months short of his hundredth birthday. He told me that in the 90 years since he had made that promise to his father in the barn, he had kept his word. Coaching is a profession that is often known for its profanity and coarse language, but Coach John Wooden rose above that and taught his players to do the same.

He shared with me about a time that his UCLA Bruins were the visiting team, and they were meeting in their locker room in an arena across the country. One of the janitors for the building had come into the locker room and used some profanity. Coach Wooden stopped the meeting and politely said, "Sir, could you please watch your language." The janitor was quite surprised, being used to such language being acceptable in the locker room, and asked, "Are there ladies present?" Coach Wooden responded, "No, sir. There are no ladies present, but hopefully there are a number of gentlemen."

What you say tells others what you know. How you say it tells them who you are. You can disagree verbally without being disagreeable. It is important to never attack another person. When it is necessary, you must challenge the other person's behavior. In this way, we would never call a person a liar. We would, instead, challenge the truth of a specific statement they have made.

Try to make every statement in such a way that you would feel comfortable being quoted directly, both now and far into the future.

As you go through the day today, pay attention to not only what you say but how you say it.

*Today's the day!*

# Happy Birthday

T HE UNITED STATES CELEBRATES ITS BIRTHDAY ON THE 4TH OF
July with fireworks, family, friends, food, and a midsummer
holiday. It is important to remember why we celebrate.

The United States of America is a beacon of hope and possibility for people around the world. As a government of the people, by the people, and for the people, we are imperfect because we are people. We make mistakes, we disagree, and we debate, but like any other family, we have always pulled together and united whenever confronted or threatened.

Election cycles leave a lot of Americans disappointed and disillusioned. It is important, though, that we focus our feelings of discontent into positive and productive pursuits. If you did not like the last election results, midterm campaigns are already organizing, providing you with an outlet for your efforts and energy.

Democracy is an exercise in compromise, which inevitably means that no one gets all of what they want, but all of us get some of what we want. Just as in our legal system, we derive our closest version of truth and justice by having a jury of citizens evaluate and decide between two opposing positions, our government functions best when the various factions work out their differences in the public forum.

Democracy is never efficient, clean, nor streamlined, but it is the best chance we humans have to provide everyone with life, liberty, and the pursuit of happiness. You can find a smooth, efficiently-running government in North Korea. For example, a completely new policy can be imagined in the morning, drafted during the day, and implemented by nightfall. There will be no debate, dissent, or dispute—but I can't imagine anyone in America wanting to trade our turmoil for that brand of false tranquility.

Even in the midst of the most turbulent political process in recent memory, this grand ideal we call America worked well. Our greatness is symbolized and lived out when one administration relinquishes control and voluntarily turns it over to an incoming administration even though the two groups may be polar opposites and diametrically opposed to one another. Our system is not always comfortable or attractive. It is simply the best one the world has ever known.

As you go through your day today, celebrate what America is and what it can be.

*Today's the day!*

# EVERYDAY WISDOM

WHEN WE STUDY HISTORY, IT MAY APPEAR THAT THERE ARE only a handful of really critical days. These days would be considered turning points and might include the bombing of Pearl Harbor, the day President Kennedy was shot, the day of the moon landing, and many other notable milestones in history. In reality, there are countless episodes over many days that led up to each of those historic dates.

The same is true in our lives. Our scrapbooks may be filled with memorabilia surrounding graduations, weddings, awards, and all manner of our own achievements, but in reality, many days go into a graduation, a wedding, a business success, or a championship.

As an Olympic weightlifter myself, I have always been fascinated with the day of competition. People from around the world tune in to watch athletes perform on a specific day; however, many months, years, or even decades go into each of those performances. I would argue that each of those days of training is just as important as the day of competition. We will be known for the consistent things we do on days that we would call "normal days" as much as we are known for the turning-point days. In fact, the everyday things we do give us the opportunity to compete or perform on those turning-point historic days.

There are activities we should endeavor to make a part of our daily routine that will culminate in us having a great life. Howard W. Hunter may have compiled one of the best lists of these daily activities. He said every day we should, *"Mend a quarrel. Seek out a forgotten friend. Dismiss suspicion and replace it with trust. Write a letter. Give a soft answer. Encourage youth. Manifest your loyalty in word and deed. Keep a promise, forego a grudge, forgive an enemy. Apologize. Try to understand. Examine your demands on others. Think first of someone else. Be kind. Be gentle. Laugh a little more. Express your gratitude. Welcome a stranger. Gladden the heart of a child. Take pleasure in the beauty and wonder of the earth. Speak your love, and speak it again."*

Feel free to add your own daily activities to Mr. Hunter's list. If you will treat every day as if it were a gift, and perform daily as if you were in the Olympics, you will have a great life.

As you go through your day today, remember that every action, relationship, and activity matters.

*Today's the day!*

# THINK AND GROW RICH MOVIE

I F YOU WERE TO ASK THE MOST SUCCESSFUL PEOPLE IN THE world in business, sports, politics, or any other arena of life what single book and author has been most instrumental in their success, you would inevitably hear *Think and Grow Rich* by Napoleon Hill more than any other answer. I am very excited to be involved both onscreen and behind the scenes in the *Think and Grow Rich* movie project.

You, along with your family, friends, and colleagues, can get involved with this monumental project from the ground up. Visit www.ThinkAndGrowRichTheMovie.com. I remain convinced that if literary giants such as Shakespeare, Mark Twain, Ernest Hemingway, or Napoleon Hill were alive today, they would not only be writing more books, but they would also be presenting their messages via motion pictures. I have more than 10 million books in print, but I remain keenly aware that there are countless people around the world who will never receive my message through the printed word but will get it via the silver screen.

Napoleon Hill was born in the 19th century, made his contribution to humanity in the 20th century, and remains one of the most influential figures in the 21st century. Any person, particularly pioneers, can only be judged against the backdrop of the time and place in which they lived. Orville and Wilbur Wright's historic flight only lasted a few seconds and traveled less than the length of a football field, but it forever changed the world in which we live.

Any success or personal development author, including myself, who has written a book in the past 75 years invariably owes a debt of gratitude to Napoleon Hill. The wisdom and perspective I am able to share through my weekly columns, my books, the motion pictures based on them, as well as my speeches are only possible because I, like all of my colleagues in the success field, stand on the shoulders of giants like Napoleon Hill.

Christopher Columbus, Daniel Boone, Neil Armstrong, and Napoleon Hill have indelibly made their mark in history not only for where they took us but because they were the first to brave the elements and go where no one had been before.

As you go through your day today, learn from the masters and get involved with the *Think and Grow Rich* movie.

*Today's the day!*

# ANYTHING AND EVERYTHING

COMPARTMENTALIZATION OF THE VARIOUS COMPONENTS IN our lives may be a good planning tool, but the various elements of our lives do not exist independently. The way you do anything is the way you will do everything.

Winning and success are habits as are losing and failure. Anything worth doing is worth doing to the highest level of excellence. Never assume that a job or task is so insignificant that you can give it a halfhearted effort. That halfhearted effort will begin to define who you are and impact every area of your life.

My late, great friend and mentor Coach John Wooden often told his players, "You will be known for a lifetime of great things you do or one lapse in judgment."

As my colleague and former NBA player, Jim King, told me, "A leader is a leader all the time." A leader is who you are, not what you do. Leaders are people who are, quite simply, worthy of following. Everyone gets to select those individuals they will look upon as leaders. Whether it's a corporate executive, a politician, a member of the clergy, or a teacher, the image of being a leader takes decades to build and can be demolished by a few misguided acts in one day.

My good friend, Steve Dubin, introduced me to a concept he used to make himself successful in business and in life. Steve calls it *Role Model Conduct* which is simply performing in a manner that will create success for you and anyone who emulates your conduct.

We need look no further than Richard Nixon or Lance Armstrong to see examples of people who succeeded at the highest level and became leaders to millions who were later disappointed by a brief lapse in judgment or conduct. Success doesn't provide days off. Even during their vacation or weekend leisure time, people look to leaders and role models to provide examples of behavior and paths to success.

I do quite a bit of work on television and two live radio broadcasts each week. Being live on the air requires an individual to use appropriate language, conversation, and dialogue. This is much easier to accomplish for those professional broadcasters who conduct themselves in an appropriate manner all the time. The favorite son of my home state of Oklahoma, Will Rogers, may have said it best. "Live your life in such a way that you wouldn't mind selling the family parrot to the town gossip."

Young people you may think are totally ignoring you may not catch all of the lessons you are trying to impart to them, but they will somehow be able to quote word-for-word anything you say that is profane or inappropriate.

The connectivity in our society means that we are called upon to interact with virtually everyone in the world. We will be judged by our words and our demeanor long before anyone examines our performance.

As you go through your day today, do the right thing next and the next thing right.

*Today's the day!*

# FAITH AND INTELLECT

**I** HAVE LONG BEEN IN THE HABIT OF READING A BOOK EACH DAY. As a blind person, this is possible due to high-speed audiobooks. Early in my studies, I believed that being spiritual and being intellectual were two different pursuits. Then I discovered the writings of C. S. Lewis. If you ever meet anyone who tells you that you can't have faith and an extraordinary intellect at the same time, simply suggest they read any book written by C. S. Lewis. As an avid reader and writer, I will not try to paraphrase or even comment upon Mr. Lewis's work, but I will, instead, allow his own words to speak for themselves.

"Adventures are never fun while you're having them."

"True humility is not thinking less of yourself; it is thinking of yourself less."

"Education without values, as useful as it is, seems rather to make man a more clever devil."

"Hardship often prepares an ordinary person for an extraordinary destiny."

"We are what we believe we are."

"Even in literature and art, no man who bothers about originality will ever be original: whereas if you simply try to tell the truth (without caring two pence how often it has been told before) you will, nine times out of ten, become original without ever having noticed it."

"With the possible exception of the equator, everything begins somewhere."

"What you see and hear depends a great deal on where you are standing. It also depends on what sort of person you are."

"Experience: that most brutal of teachers. But you learn; my God, do you learn."

"We meet no ordinary people in our lives."

"The homemaker has the ultimate career. All other careers exist for one purpose only—and that is to support the ultimate career."

"We all want progress, but if you're on the wrong road, progress means doing an about-turn and walking back to the right road; in that case, the man who turns back soonest is the most progressive."

"Integrity is doing the right thing, even when no one is watching."

"Failures, repeated failures, are finger posts on the road to achievement. One fails forward toward success."

Spirituality, faith, intellect, and education can all live together and coexist quite nicely. In fact, once we are exposed to great thought leaders such as C. S. Lewis, we begin to understand that they not only don't contradict each other, they are interdependent.

As you go through your day today, read more, learn more, and believe more.

*Today's the day!*

# PAYING IT FORWARD

ONE OF THE INTERESTING RESULTS OF WRITING CLOSE TO 40 books and having eight of them thus far turned into movies is the fact that every few months when one of the new offerings is released, I get to do a lot of TV, print, and radio interviews.

I had a second interview with Rick Young who hosts a live program in New York City called *What's in Your Hand* on 90.3 FM. If you're in the New York area, I highly recommend you check it out. Rick's show focuses on success, possibilities, and making our lives everything they should be. I was scheduled to do only a 20-minute interview to discuss my new book being released, but it went so well, and Rick kept asking me to stay on, so we ended up doing an hour-and-a-half.

At the end of the program on live radio broadcast throughout New York City, Rick asked if I would do him a favor. I took a deep breath and a leap of faith as I simply replied that I would, not knowing what he might ask me to do. Rick told me that sometime during that very day, he wanted me to do a random act of kindness for someone who didn't expect it and for which I would receive nothing in return. After the program, I thought about it, and it wasn't long before someone visited my office, and I gave them an autographed copy of one of my novels. My guest thanked me, and I told them that if there was any thanks due, it wasn't to me, but it instead, was to a radio host in New York.

My guest thought that was really amazing, and as the person left my office with the book, the person promised to do their own random act of kindness for someone else.

I realized that we're all planting seeds every day. Not only in our own lives, but in the lives of people around us. These seeds don't add. They multiply. So if you do something for someone else and they pass it on, by the end of the day, the random act of kindness that you have paid forward could touch the lives of thousands of people. When we do things for others not expecting to benefit, we inevitably receive a mental and spiritual benefit, but often we also receive an unexpected benefit.

I am very grateful that I have become among the highest paid convention speakers in the country. As my own way of maintaining balance and giving back to society, I try to do one speech for free for each speech where I am paid. Last year, I had the privilege of speaking at a wonderful corporate event in Maui, Hawaii, for which I was exceedingly well paid. After the event, I asked the president of that organization how they had learned about me and why they had hired me. The president let me know that he had never heard of me and was unaware of my work, but his 10-year-old granddaughter told him about when I came to her fifth-grade class to talk to the kids. So while I was trying to give some of my time and energy to some kids in a classroom, I was planting the seed that would result in thousands of dollars and a wonderful professional opportunity.

Success comes when we plant seeds and don't worry about how or when we will get paid.

As you go through your day today, pay it forward, and you will make a difference for others as well as yourself.

*Today's the day!*

# STALKING THE ELEPHANT

MANY PEOPLE WOULD CLAIM TO BELIEVE THAT *ANYTHING* is possible, but when it comes to their own life, career, and success, they don't believe *everything* is possible.

The concept of anything being possible is random and ethereal. It includes ideas such as "I might win the lottery," "We might get hit by a meteor," or "If I'm lucky, I could get the perfect job and meet Mr. or Miss Right." In these examples, believing in anything being possible assumes that the outcome is not within our control but it's possible. On the other hand, when we believe that we control our destiny and our fate is in our own hands, we understand that everything is open to us based on the choices we make and how hard we want to work.

I am an entrepreneur and run a small business called the Narrative Television Network. Due to a lot of hard work by our team, we landed a contract to do business with one of the largest corporations in the world. Many well-meaning, well-intentioned, and knowledgeable people would assert that a little company from Oklahoma with less than ten employees couldn't do business on a level playing field with a multinational, multibillion-dollar giant. In reality, if they believe it's impossible in their circumstances, they are right. If I believe it's possible for our team, I'm right.

Success is a self-fulfilling prophecy. In my book *The Million-aire Map,* I explain that if you want to be successful, you need to surround yourself with a group of people who have what you want. I call these people your Dream Team. I'm a firm believer in being willing to be turned down or rejected by the very best. At the start of any endeavor, if you will simply believe that everything is possible and open to you, you can list the candidates for your Dream Team.

When we started the Narrative Television Network, we had no background, training, experience, or resources in the industry. When I asked myself, "If I could have anyone I wanted on my Dream Team to advise and assist us, who would I pick?" The answer was as simple to me then as it is now. Ted Turner. When we got involved in the financial planning and investment arena, the potential Dream Team member I listed first was Steve Forbes. When we got into the field of leadership training, the first name that came to my mind of someone I wanted on our side was the legendary Coach John Wooden. When my novels began to be sought for movie projects and I was looking for people on my Dream Team, I thought of people like James Garner, Peter Fonda, Raquel Welch, and Academy Award-winner Louis Gossett Jr. I am pleased to report that each of these special people has contributed and continues to contribute to our success. As ancient wisdom tells us, "You have not because you ask not."

As you go through your day today, set your sights high, and you might just get what you aim at.

***Today's the day!***

# WHAT'S IN A NAME?

I READ A NEWS STORY ABOUT THE NAME OF A STREET BEING changed in my hometown. The street had been named after one of the founding fathers in the city many decades ago, but apparently, some research uncovered the fact that the namesake of this street had held some political or social views that are currently out-of-favor. Then several weeks later, another news story appeared announcing that the name on a building at the law school on the campus of a local university was being taken down because the namesake of the building who had been a benefactor to the university had, for a short period of time over a half-century ago, been a member of a political group that espoused some views that are out-of-favor here in the twenty-first century.

Often in the midst of a heated political campaign, voters lament the fact that there doesn't seem to be any qualified candidates on the ballot. The reality is that none of us are perfect, and no one can stand up to the harsh light of criticism throughout their entire life.

I have read several thousand biographies of people I greatly admire and people of historical significance. I have learned a great deal from the lives of Leonardo da Vinci, Benjamin Franklin, Thomas Jefferson, Margaret Thatcher, Franklin Roosevelt, and Mother Teresa; but none of these outstanding individuals could stand up to the scrutiny that caused the names to be changed on a local street and a local building in my hometown.

Gandhi said that every person is my superior in that I can learn something from them. One of my favorite authors, Louis L'Amour, often wrote, "No one can be judged except against the backdrop of the time and place in which they lived."

If we expect our heroes, politicians, and philanthropists to be perfect, we will have no one to look up to, no candidates on the ballots, and no generous donations to worthy organizations. We should judge our everyday deeds and actions like we would look at a snapshot. It freezes a certain moment in time, but the totality of someone's life should be judged like a great motion picture.

As mentioned previously, I have written almost 40 books. To date, eight of them have been turned into movies. I am very proud of all these films, but none of them are perfect. Film editors, sound engineers, and digital technicians work for months after a movie is shot to make it the best it can be, but it is never perfect.

We need to hold ourselves to the highest ideals of our own standards and allow other people's legacies to speak for themselves within the perspective of time and history.

As you go through your day today, be the best you can be, and look for the best in everyone else.

*Today's the day!*

# REMEMBERING THE CHAMP

IN 2016, THE WHOLE WORLD MOURNED THE LOSS OF Muhammad Ali. He was arguably exactly what he told us he was: "The greatest of all times." This would be more than enough for any one person's life, but if you only consider Ali as a boxer, you would miss the majority of who he was and the impact he had on the world.

I met Ali briefly once, but I came to know and understand him best, ironically, from talking with two of his opponents. In any other era of boxing, George Foreman or Joe Frazier would have been dominant, but in the era of Ali, they paled in comparison both in and out of the ring. Both Frazier and Foreman had been bitter rivals of Ali but came to love and respect him as a champion and a friend.

Although it has been more than 30 years since the last time Muhammad Ali appeared in a boxing ring, he remained one of the world's most recognized and beloved figures.

I believe the best tribute I can offer for the champ is to allow him to do what he did so well throughout his life which was to simply speak for himself. The following are a few of my favorite Ali quotes:

"A man who views the world the same at 50 as he did at 20 has wasted 30 years of his life."

"Service to others is the rent you pay for your room here on earth."

"Don't count the days. Make the days count."

"It isn't the mountains ahead to climb that wear you out. It's the pebble in your shoe."

*Muhamed Ali*

"I am the greatest. I said that even before I knew I was."

"Only a man who knows what it is like to be defeated can reach down to the bottom of his soul and come up with the extra ounce of power it takes to win when the match is even."

"He who is not courageous enough to take risks will accomplish nothing in life."

"*Impossible* is just a big word thrown around by small men who find it easier to live in the world they've been given than to explore the power they have to change it. *Impossible* is not a fact. It's an opinion. *Impossible* is not a declaration. It's a dare. *Impossible* is potential. *Impossible* is temporary. *Impossible* is nothing."

As you go through your day today, remember one more quote from the champ. "Live every day as if it were your last because someday you're going to be right."

***Today's the day!***

# SIGNS OF SUCCESS

# THE ULTIMATE LEGACY

I HAVE WRITTEN ALMOST 40 BOOKS TO DATE; AND AT THIS writing, eight of them have been turned into movies with others being planned for the future. Having a book published is a gift and an honor. To consider that people around the world should spend their hard-earned money and their valuable time with one of my books is a supreme compliment and a distinct privilege. Then to even imagine one of those books turned into a major motion picture in which a character who was nothing more than a figment of my imagination comes to life 30 feet tall on movie screens around the world is difficult to even contemplate.

*The Ultimate Legacy* movie—based on my book *The Gift of a Legacy*—was released in theatres and was broadcast on the *Hallmark* network in 2015. *The Ultimate Legacy* is the third film in *The Ultimate Gift* trilogy. Anyone around the world who is familiar with my work at all probably knows of me because of a little novel I wrote entitled *The Ultimate Gift* and the subsequent movie of the same name. *The Ultimate Gift* starred James Garner; the story continued in the second book and movie *The Ultimate Life* starring Peter Fonda; and *The Ultimate Legacy* starred Raquel Welch.

Everyone builds our legacy one day at a time. Often we think of a legacy as something elderly people contemplate at the end of their lives, but our legacy is our life's work that is projected into the impact it has on other people and generations to come.

Every time we are presented with a choice, it generally involves considering what will make us happy now—as opposed to what will make us content later. Invariably, the best choices involve long-term contentment instead of immediate gratification, but we can take it one step further and consider our legacy.

Success comes when we realize life is not just about us but involves others around us. Legacy takes it one step further and introduces the consideration of impacting people we may never know and generations not yet born. If we focus on our own gratification, we make poor decisions; if we think of others, we make good decisions; but if we contemplate our permanent legacy, we can approach greatness.

As you go through your day today, I hope you will share *The Ultimate Legacy* with those you care about.

**Today's the day!**

# THE ART OF COMMUNICATION

I N 2016, I WAS ONCE AGAIN GOING THROUGH THE LITERARY birthing process for my book, *The Art of Communication.* You can get a complementary sample of this title at www .JimStovallBooks.com.

*The Art of Communication* is a collaboration between me and my coauthor Ray Hull, PhD, who is one of the leading authorities on listening, hearing, and communication. I met Dr. Hull at a U.S. Department of Education conference in Washington, DC, where we both were presenting. Dr. Hull is a professor and focuses much of his work on hearing and communication disorders. As a blind person myself, it would appear that Ray and I have little in common, but the combination of his academic prowess and my real-world trial and error experience has created a powerful book we titled *The Art of Communication.*

No one succeeds in a vacuum. The great poet John Donne, in his epic work *For Whom the Bell Tolls,* shares with countless people around the world that no person is an island, and we are all interdependent. If success is, indeed, a joint effort, the ability to effectively communicate our goals and visions becomes imperative. As I often share with aspiring speakers and my colleagues in the National Speakers Association, just because you're talking doesn't mean anyone is listening. And just because they're listening doesn't mean they're hearing. And just because they're hearing doesn't mean they're understanding. And even if they understand, it doesn't mean they are understanding what you meant to communicate.

The goal of communication at its best is understanding. Two minds become one and share the same vision, goals, and destiny. Although it's asked millions of times each day, the most ridiculous question ever uttered is "Do you understand?" Every person who misunderstands and is laboring under a false impression assumes they have understood and will answer, "Yes" to the simple question "Do you understand?" If you want to change your life both personally and professionally, stop asking, "Do you understand?" and begin inquiring, "What do you understand?"

Communication is complex, and understanding is not absolute. All of us have had the experience of rereading a powerful passage in a book multiple times and understanding a bit more of the original message with each reading.

As an author, columnist, speaker, radio personality, television executive, and movie producer, I am keenly aware of the fact that the same message can impact different people in different ways depending upon the medium of communication utilized. I believe that we are all only one great idea away from success, but any great idea will languish in obscurity if we can't powerfully and passionately communicate.

As you go through your day today, remember that success is available to those who can master the art of communication.

*Today's the day!*

# What You Do with What You Have

E FFICIENCY AND PRODUCTIVITY CAN OFFSET AND OVERCOME virtually any disability, deficiency, or shortfall. College graduates with degrees in engineering make $4.8 million over their careers while early childhood education graduates make $1.4 million throughout their working lives. This would seem to indicate that anyone who wants to succeed financially should gravitate toward a career in engineering as opposed to teaching. While this is logical, it would not be my advice.

I recommend everyone pursue their passion both in their personal and their professional lives. While it is true that school teachers earn less than engineers, I personally know public school teachers who have become multimillionaires through diligent saving and investing, while you won't have to look very hard to find engineers who seem to be able to master virtually any mathematical problem except their own finances.

The pursuit of money is a road that leads to dissatisfaction and, quite often, financial ruin. The pursuit of passion invariably leads to happiness, satisfaction, and financial success. There are people who are succeeding in every field of endeavor while there is no career path that guarantees success.

As mentioned previously, six of the books I've written have been turned into major motion pictures. I have played a cameo role in each of these movies. In the first several films, I was a limo driver, but in the most recent movie—due to the fact we had a multimillion dollar limo with Raquel Welch riding in the back—I made my movie debut as a bartender.

Because of these insignificant screen roles, I had to become a member of the Screen Actors Guild. If you were to ask people randomly to describe individuals who pursue professions that make them rich, you would undoubtedly hear about movie stars, athletes, and recording artists. As a union cardholder, I can tell you that the average member of the Screen Actors Guild, which represents the elite people in the profession who have acted in at least one movie or TV show, earns less than $1,000 per year.

We all hear about the astronomical salaries in the NFL, NBA, and Major League Baseball; however, these salary numbers only apply to the top fraction of a percent of athletes who pursue a career in those sports. While there are a relative handful of fabulously wealthy recording artists, the rock star lifestyle is only a myth for the vast majority of gifted and talented musicians. While I would never discourage anyone from a career in entertainment, sports, or music, I would warn everyone against pursuing these professions or any other based on an expectation of wealth and riches.

As a professional speaker, I have many people contact me who want to join our profession. They have invariably heard about the lofty speaking fees. While I am blessed to earn more money for an hour onstage than the annual income of the average family that lives in my home state, it's important to remember that I made hundreds of speeches for free before I got paid; and had I been pursuing the speaking profession as a road to wealth, I would have quit years before I reached the promised land.

As you go through your day today, pursue your passion instead of money, and you will have both.

*Today's the day!*

# MAINTAIN YOUR EQUIPMENT

I'M A HUGE BASEBALL FAN AND ENJOY FOLLOWING GAMES throughout the season via satellite radio. One season, the Chicago Cubs performed at an extremely high level and were very competitive in the playoffs. Even longtime Cub fans would have to admit it was not the normal expectation for the Chicago Cubs. Winning seasons are not the norm, and playoff appearances are rare.

After the playoffs, the Chicago Cubs' manager was discussing elements of their season that he felt contributed to their outstanding performance. He explained one of the new strategies he interjected was not taking as much batting practice before games. This runs contrary to the generally-accepted policy within the baseball community. As a rule, teams take extensive batting practice before a game, and players who are in a slump and have not been hitting well spend even more time before the game in the batting cage.

The Cubs' manager felt that fatigue had set in, and they were losing focus, so he got his team out of the longtime ritual of lengthy batting practice prior to games. The strategy obviously worked for the Chicago Cubs, and I believe it can work for you and me in our lives and careers.

People read my weekly columns in many countries around the world, but in the United States, working extra hours, eliminating days off, and overextending ourselves have become some kind of badge of honor. I hear people in the workplace bragging about how tired they are, how many days in a row they've worked, and how little vacation they have taken. In the Japanese work culture, it is actually considered a bad practice and viewed as cheating your company if you overwork, therefore becoming tired and less effective. Japanese workers who do not take all of their vacations are looked upon like equipment, buildings, or other assets not properly cared for and maintained.

For many years, I have had a policy in my company and with the people who work in my ventures that, barring some kind of emergency, we don't work extra hours or weekends. It's important to note that we haven't had one of these types of emergencies in many years. It's not that our people aren't dedicated. I'll put my team up against anybody in the world. It's simply a matter of good management and taking care of our number one asset— our workforce. If you want to take care of your business and take care of your family, start by taking care of yourself.

As you go through your day today, realize that recreation and relaxation are critical parts of your success.

*Today's the day!*

# THE FIVE FACTOR

AMONG THE MOST SIGNIFICANT DISCOVERIES IN THE FIELD OF human success and achievement in the past quarter century is the understanding that we become like the five people with whom we spend the most time. Humans are very social and impressionable creatures. We have a tendency to be influenced by everyone around us, but most significantly, we are impacted by the five people in our inner circle. Whether they are friends, family members, or colleagues, the five people in our immediate environment the majority of the time have the greatest influence upon us.

Further studies have shown that our income and financial net worth will approach the average of the five people we are in contact with the most. This does not mean we shouldn't spend time with and even serve those who are less fortunate. It simply means we need to be aware of the people who have an influence upon us.

In my book *The Millionaire Map,* in which I recount my own journey from poverty to wealth, I discuss in detail the concept of developing a "dream team." As discussed previously, your dream team is made up of the people you would most want around you in any venture or endeavor. They would be people with the greatest name recognition, experience, and expertise within the arena where you are competing. For example, when

I was an athlete, I was trained for several years by an Olympic champion. His success, his habits, and his competitive nature rubbed off on me.

As you read in a previous entry, my dream team consisted of Ted Turner, Steve Forbes, Academy Award-winner Louis Gossett Jr., James Garner, Peter Fonda, Raquel Welch, and many others. Please understand I've been turned down and ignored by many people whom I wanted on my dream team or in my inner circle, but at least I reached out to them. If you ask someone to be a part of your dream team, they might tell you no, but if you don't ask them, I can guarantee the answer is no.

As you go through your day today, remember the five factor, and choose wisely.

*Today's the day!*

# SECOND CHANCES

I'M A FIRM BELIEVER THAT IT IS NEVER AS BAD AS IT MAY LOOK, and there are always alternatives, possibilities, and second chances. As the late, great sage Yogi Berra said, "It ain't over 'til it's over."

For many years, the Empire State Building in New York City was the tallest building in the world. It remains an iconic structure today and has been immortalized in many legends, movies, and television programs. Over the decades, more than 30 people have jumped from the extreme height of the Empire State Building. Few things in the course of human endeavor would seem more hopeless and final than leaping from the Empire State Building to end one's life; however, history reveals that on two occasions, people with every intention of committing suicide jumped from a height of nearly 1,000 feet and lived to tell about it.

In 1979, a woman jumped from the 86th floor of the Empire State Building, but instead of plunging to the pavement nearly a quarter of a mile below, she was blown into an open window on a lower floor. She suffered a broken hip but, otherwise, received a second chance at life.

In 2013, a man jumped from the observation deck, but once again instead of ending his life, he was found on a window ledge beneath where he had jumped, the beneficiary of another favorable wind.

All of us have had failures and setbacks. Some of them are random, and others we have brought on ourselves. Success and failure are defined by each individual and are not final until we declare it so. The history books are filled with people who suffered the most devastating failures imaginable and experienced great success that followed.

In early 2000, I was contacted by Steve Forbes. He wanted to feature me, along with approximately a dozen other businesspeople, in a book he titled *Great Success Stories*. I was privileged to be included alongside Mr. Forbes, Donald Trump, Tom Monaghan, and other iconic business leaders. But the subtitle of the book reveals the true story: *Twelve Tales of Victory Wrested from Defeat*. It is ironic that initial failure doesn't preclude long-term success. In fact, in many cases, failures and setbacks become the launching pad for great success.

If you've experienced failure, you need to explore what you have learned, how you have grown, and the lessons you have internalized. When you take inventory, you may realize that it's not a matter of you starting over—it's a matter of the new and improved you getting another chance.

As you go through your day today, remember that failure isn't final. It's fertilizer for success.

*Today's the day!*

# WORDS TO LIVE BY

OUR LIVES ARE PRODUCTS OF OUR THOUGHTS AND BELIEFS. We become what we think about and believe in. The only vehicle we have to communicate our thoughts and beliefs is the words we use.

Occasionally, I run across a statement of someone's thoughts or beliefs that seems absurd or impossible, but upon further reflection, I realize must be true. I remember reading a quote from Mother Teresa: "Unless you love everyone unconditionally, you don't really love anyone at all." This seems like it can't be true and it must be true all at the same time.

I read a powerful quote from Gandhi that I am still trying to assimilate into my mind and into my life. Gandhi said, "Unless you can find God in the next person you meet, you need look no further." I believe Gandhi was challenging us to find goodness, love, and light in everyone. While sometimes this seems impossible, I believe it's imperative, and furthermore, I believe unless we can find happiness, fun, significance, or opportunity in the next person we meet, we need look no further.

In our fast-paced world of instant media sound bites, it is easy to prejudge and dismiss a person based on one fault or flaw that can't escape the media glare. We need to measure people based on the totality of their lives, not a single unfortunate incident, minor mistake, or lapse of judgment.

My mentor and friend the late, great Coach John Wooden who rewrote the college basketball record books and established championship numbers that may never be equaled, was fond of saying, "There's enough good in the worst of us, and enough bad in the best of us, that it doesn't behoove any of us to judge anyone." While I agree with the admonition that we should not judge others, we are encouraged to examine the fruit in their lives. Judging people only needs an instantaneous impression, while examining the fruit in their lives takes a long and thoughtful process.

Too often, our tendency is to judge everyone else's actions while judging our own intentions. This will always lead to a skewed worldview. Excellence comes when we hold ourselves to the highest standard while allowing others an extra measure of grace.

As you go through your day today, control your thoughts and beliefs, and find words to live by.

*Today's the day!*

# LOST AND FOUND

$A$S A GENERAL RULE, HAVING A GREAT MEMORY IS A wonderful tool that can help you succeed in any area of life. There are a number of books and courses designed to help you improve your memory or better utilize the memory you have. There's no reason to clutter your mind or memory capacity with data that can be stored on a computer or handheld device.

A generation ago, people routinely remembered dozens of phone numbers and could recall them in an instant and then dial the phone. Today, smart phones eliminate the need to memorize anyone's phone number. I've been in the company of extremely intelligent people who actually had to look up their own phone number because they rarely, if ever, have to remember it and dial it manually. GPS technology makes it possible for us to get anywhere in the world without remembering how to get there or how to get back home.

One of the greatest benefits of an accurate memory has always been and remains the ability to remember people's names. Few things are more valuable to any person than their own name, and if you can readily recall someone's name, you are miles ahead of someone who can't remember an individual's name.

With all the benefits of having and using a great memory, there is at least one case in which successful people cultivate the skill of *not* remembering. Great professional quarterbacks who have just thrown an interception develop the ability to put the mistake out of their mind and go back out on the field for the next series without letting the interception impact their thinking or their play. Great pitchers who just watched the opposing team's batter hit the ball over the fence are in the habit of shaking it off, taking a deep breath, and getting back to business with the next batter as if the homerun never happened.

You and I have had times in our lives and careers when we succeeded and other times when we failed. Those among us who perform consistently at the highest level are those who remember their victories and forget their defeats. When faced with a crisis or the proverbial fork in the road, remember to go back and mentally review all of your victories before you proceed. Any of us have experienced enough victories to think of ourselves as a winner or enough defeats to think of ourselves as a loser.

Always choose to identify yourself as a winner, and mentally go back to the last time you won. Then assume that attitude and strategy. This is how the winners stay on top.

As you go through your day today, remember the great things, and forget the rest.

*Today's the day!*

# PRACTICE AND PERFECTION

URING THE SUMMER OF 2016, BILLIONS OF PEOPLE AROUND
D the globe watched the myriad of competitions in the
Olympic games. As a former Olympic weightlifter, I follow the
Olympics every four years with great interest. No one would
argue that great athletes are a result of countless hours of practice, but the question has arisen in recent research as to whether
all people start at the same place in learning a skill or sport.

One of the fun things about having six of my books turned
into movies with several others in the works is the privilege of
working with some great musicians. In addition to my talented
colleague Kelly Morrison who has written and/or recorded songs
for each of the films based on my novels, we've been able to
include music from Willie Nelson, Bob Dylan, Aaron Copeland,
Patsy Cline, and the legendary B.B. King. B.B. King's amazing
musical career was the basis for curiosity that has resulted in
some psychological studies that can impact you and me.

B.B. King described how—as a very small boy—he happened onto his uncle's guitar and began picking out some tunes.
Scientists recently conducted a study of 15 adults to determine
their ability to learn and master music. As these scientists mea-
sured different parts of the participants' brains, they discovered
that some people who displayed what we might call "natural talent" had a very active parietal cortex and premotor cortex within

their brains. The research revealed that all participants could learn music and improve their skills with practice, but some people had more innate talent or gifts for performing music than others.

In his groundbreaking book *Outliers*, Malcolm Gladwell developed the theory that 10,000 hours of study or practice in any field can produce mastery. While this may be true, the research clearly indicates that not all brains are created equally, and people may have more aptitude for some activities than others.

I have long believed that the meaning of life is to find our gift, and then we achieve purpose and significance when we give it away. Parents, teachers, coaches, managers, and executives need to remember that a great team is made up of individual people performing in the position of their greatest talent and ability for the overall good.

As you go through your day today, find your place and perform with excellence.

*Today's the day!*

# AVOIDING DECISIONS

O UR DAILY LIVES ARE MADE UP OF LITERALLY THOUSANDS OF individual decisions. Many of these decisions we make automatically, while others we ignore resulting in our decisions being made for us.

One of the human traits that invariably results in failure is the habit of avoiding decisions. The concept of avoiding decisions is absurd. It simply doesn't exist. Not making a decision is a decision. When we put off a decision or avoid it altogether, our options are narrowed or eliminated entirely.

Recently I ran into an acquaintance of mine at an event where I was speaking. He told me that he had moved into a lake development near the city where we live. When I asked him about his new house on the lake, he told me his house was not located on the water and didn't have a very good view because he was one of the last owners to build a house. Then he went on to explain the key to opportunity, success, and happiness for you and me. My acquaintance told me he had been approached by the lakefront developer before the lots went up for sale to the general public. He could have had his pick of any of the lots, many of which were situated right on the lakeshore with magnificent views; but he explained he couldn't make up his mind and delayed his decision until the only lot left was in an obscure, undesirable corner of the development.

Delaying a decision diminishes our choices. Avoiding a decision entirely transfers our right to choose to someone else; but never forget, we always live with our decisions whether we make them promptly or avoid them entirely.

The great parliamentarian Edmund Burke said, "The only thing necessary for the triumph of evil is for good men to do nothing." If we choose not to get involved, we are deciding to keep things the way they are or allow them to decline further. If we don't vote, we are giving our precious right and freedom over to others who will elect our leaders and form policy for future generations.

We all fight the fear of making a bad or wrong decision. It's important to remember that even a bad decision is preferable to not deciding. At least you're in control of your fate and can change course and get back on the right track.

The world belongs to those who will make a decision and stick with it.

As you go through your day today, explore all possibilities and exercise your right to choose.

*Today's the day!*

# Just Say No

SUCCESS IN BUSINESS, FINANCES, OR LIFE IN GENERAL COMES from making good decisions. Good decisions are products of saying yes to the right things that require us to say no to everything else. This is simple but never easy.

Once you begin having some success, a myriad of people and organizations will begin to request your time and money. Your time is the most valuable commodity you have. Unlike money or virtually any other possession, time can never be replaced, so we must spend it wisely.

At this stage of my life and career, if I said yes to all requests for a speech or an appearance, I would literally be traveling somewhere every day. The majority of these requests are for good causes, but if I am going to pursue my own mission and reach my own goals, I have to say no to *good* things so that I have the time to invest in *great* things.

I received some wonderful advice from Oprah Winfrey, who you can imagine, is inundated with requests for her time and money. She said she used to make excuses or explain conflicts in her schedule, but she has learned to simply say, "No, that isn't going to work for me." I have implemented this in my life and have found it to work wonderfully.

I remember before I got the valuable advice from Oprah, I received a request from an out-of-state charity to speak at their annual banquet. This is a wonderful charity that does good work, but it would have required me to be gone for three days which would include a day of travel, the day of the appearance, and a day of travel to get home. In this same three-day investment of my time, I could help several organizations in my local community, so I told them I was busy on the day of their event. They responded by moving their annual banquet several days ahead, and I felt obligated to be there. The freedom of just saying, "No, that's not going to work for me," has eliminated many of the awkward and uncomfortable conversations.

In much the same way people request our time, they will request a loan or a gift of money. Once you have achieved a modicum of success, you lose the age-old excuse of saying, "Sorry, I don't have any money," when people hit you up for a gift or loan. Please understand I'm not talking about people who need food or medicine. I'm talking about people who have made poor decisions in their own financial lives, and they are in the habit of repeatedly asking people who have made good decisions for gifts or loans. Invariably, these people do not want to change their lives or the poor decisions they are making. They just want you to pay for their mistakes.

As logical and clear-cut as this seems, it is still difficult to say no. I have developed a response to these financial requests that is similar to Oprah's response to requests for time. When people ask for a loan or a gift of money that I do not feel is appropriate, I simply tell them, "I have budgeted all my spending, investing, and giving a year in advance, so I'm not in a position to do anything for you at this time." If you haven't already budgeted your spending, investing, and giving, do so now, and you will be in a position to say no to the inappropriate requests and to say yes to the great ones.

As you go through your day today, say no when you should, and you will be able to say yes to your future.

*Today's the day!*

# THE DOUBLE CHECKING BONUS

WE'RE ALL HUMAN, AND WE ALL MAKE MISTAKES. THE difference between the people who are great and people who are mediocre is not whether they make mistakes. It is *how* they deal with them and *when* they deal with them. Mediocre performers allow a mistake to go unobserved until it confronts a customer or end user. A great performer has a system in place that catches and corrects mistakes before anyone suffers.

Among the most costly line items in any organization's ledgers are the mistakes that are made and have to be corrected. If you send out the wrong order to a valued client, you not only have to deal with the cost of recalling what you sent and delivering the correct order, but you deal with the loss of reputation and faith that the customer no longer feels for you and your team. The measurable cost is the shipping, restocking, and accounting charges that result from the mistake. The intangible cost which may never be fully understood involves future business and referrals that you will never see.

My late, great colleague Dr. Wayne Dyer was one of the best authors and speakers of his generation. He had a vendor who shipped out all of his books and videos to corporate clients and individuals. He instructed the vendor to double check all orders, but when the inevitable mistake was made, they were to contact him personally. Dr. Dyer called each of his clients and spoke to them individually, apologizing for the mistake and letting them know he would be overnighting them the correct order, which he would personally autograph, and he would include a free copy of his latest book or video free-of-charge. Dr. Dyer had calculated that the cost of each mistake from his fulfillment vendor was approximately $100 to repair, but the cost of not repairing the mistake could mount up to many thousands of dollars in the future.

Ironically, over the past several years, I have spoken to many other authors and speakers about Dr. Dyer's policy, and many of them were already aware of it as were many corporations and organizations around the world. These inadvertent shipping mistakes turned into reputation builders and marketing opportunities as his solutions to the problems made Dr. Wayne Dyer legendary in the business world.

Some professionals such as surgeons and pilots have mandatory checklists and systems in place to avoid or immediately identify mistakes because an error in their world can be literally life and death. You and I need to build similar systems because there are few things in this world more important than our word, integrity, and reputation.

As you go through your day today, avoid the mistakes you can, and fix the others.

*Today's the day!*

# REFLECT, REFRESH, AND RENEW

DECEMBER 22 IS RELEVANT BECAUSE IT REPRESENTS A milestone day my colleagues and I observe each year. Like most entrepreneurs, I am totally committed to my business, my colleagues, and the people we serve. If we are ever to grow in our professional lives, we have to have a specific period of time when we're not working *at* our job, career, or business, but we are, instead, working *on* our job, career, or business.

If you're working *at* your job, you are performing routine tasks that are necessary in order to function at the level where you currently exist. When you're working *on* your business or job, you are thinking, developing, and being creative in ways that will extend the scope and depth of your impact.

Each year, we close our business for approximately two weeks. This gives my colleagues and me a chance to relax, renew, recommit, and think about where we've been and where we're going as opposed to the daily grind of maintaining the status quo.

I read a biography about a pope who served during the Middle Ages. He explained that before he had been selected to be the pope, he had been able to commit two hours each day to prayer and meditation so he could prepare himself for the day's work. He went on to explain that after he became pope, his schedule became so full and his duties were so overwhelming that he was forced to alter his time of prayer and meditation. You might think he cut down on his prayer and meditation time in order to commit those two hours toward his daily tasks. Ironically, he took the two hours of prayer and meditation and extended it to four hours each day so he could be prepared for his increased work load.

My late, great friend and colleague Dr. Stephen Covey, in his transformational book *The 7 Habits of Highly Effective People,* described what we must do in order to be successful. Among the most significant of Dr. Covey's seven habits is one he called *Sharpening the Saw.* He described how sometimes in order to produce more lumber, we can't just work harder and more franti-cally, but we must pause to sharpen the saw and be more efficient and productive. Our mind, emotion, intellect, and creativity rep-resent our saw. They are the tools we have that make us bigger, better, and more creative than we are. There are times when we must stop and maintain our tools if we are going to perform at a higher level.

As you go through your day today, commit to maintaining your saw and yourself.

*Today's the day!*

# PROBLEMS AND SOLUTIONS

IDEAS AND OPPORTUNITIES COME DISGUISED AS PROBLEMS. As I travel around the world and meet countless people from every walk of life, they seem to all be looking for the same discoveries or breakthroughs in their lives.

Among the most common elements sought by people is a great idea. People are convinced if they had one great idea, they could change everything in their world. This is true. We need look no farther than the business pages of our local paper to see how ideas can transform everything around us.

The only thing you have to do to put yourself in a position to have a great idea is to go through your daily routine, wait for something bad to happen, and ask yourself, "How could I have avoided that?" The answer to that question is invariably a great idea. The only thing you have to do to turn your great idea into a business opportunity is to ask yourself one further question. "How can I help other people avoid that?"

Ideas and opportunities are otherwise known as solutions. Success in life or in business comes when we can apply our solutions to other people's problems. Lest you be worried that all the world's problems are going to be solved using other people's ideas before you have an idea of your own to bring to the marketplace, it is important to know that while solutions solve problems, they also create new problems.

Throughout recorded history, human beings have sought faster and better ways to transport themselves to places where they want to go. Over a century ago, the automobile was invented. Throughout the ensuing years, the automobile has solved many transportation problems, but it has created new problems involving safety, pollution, etc. There are solutions in development today that will solve the safety and environmental problems that the automobile has created, and once those solutions are applied, they will, in turn, create problems of their own.

The value of an idea or a solution is in direct proportion to the size of the problem. If you have an idea to cure some rare, life-threatening disease, that solution will create a large opportunity, even if the disease only impacts a relatively small number of people. The opportunity is large because the solution is the difference between life and death. On the other hand, if you create a seemingly insignificant solution to a minor problem that is experienced by the majority of people, it is still a huge opportunity because—even though you've only created an App to organize everyone's shopping list or protect our cell phones or some other common situation—the number of people impacted is so great that it generates huge potential.

It has been my experience in dealing with many emerging entrepreneurs that opportunities present themselves regardless of where you are or what you're doing. What is needed is an awareness of problems and solutions. People who will succeed through inventions and innovations in the coming years are those who don't avoid problems but embrace them as opportunities.

As you go through your day today, remember that problems and solutions equal opportunity.

*Today's the day!*

# DOUBT AND CERTAINTY

IBELIEVE THAT WE ACHIEVE A HEALTHY BALANCE IN OUR personal and professional lives when we have a curious spirit and question everything while gaining all the knowledge possible and applying it in the form of wisdom. As we achieve more understanding and awareness, we possess knowledge and are constantly in a state of knowing more than we have ever known, but this knowledge comes with a fascinating byproduct which is the growing awareness of the things we don't know.

Voltaire said, "Doubt is not a pleasant condition, but certainty is an absurd one."

In the 21st century, we achieve success and build wealth by creating value in the lives of others. Most often, the value we provide is something we know as opposed to something we do. Even people who succeed in providing services, at some point on their success ladder, stop providing the service directly and train others to do it so their efforts are multiplied.

Ideally, we should always be in the position of being aware of what we know and having an awareness that there are many things we don't know. It's perfectly acceptable and even natural to not know many things, but an awareness of this ignorance is imperative. The most dangerous people I have ever met don't know what they don't know. These individuals assume they know everything which, of course, is impossible. Even if someone is a world-renowned expert and knows more about their field than anyone else, in order to succeed, they must be aware that there are many things yet to be known.

There was a time when Orville and Wilbur Wright probably knew more about aviation than anyone in the world, but if they could get a glimpse of 21$^{st}$ century air travel, they would immediately become aware that there was much they didn't know.

Gandhi said, "Every person is my superior in that I can learn something from them." Even the most naïve or ignorant person you ever meet can teach you something if only that you don't want to be naïve and ignorant. The people who make discoveries, breakthroughs, and creative quantum leaps are those who approach every day assuming there is something waiting to be known, understood, and mastered.

The legendary filmmaker Frank Capra said, "Don't follow trends. Start them." In our fast-paced, technological world, it is a mistake to pursue the state-of-the-art because by the time you get there, it will have moved ahead leaving you obsolete. This was best illustrated by Wayne Gretzky the great hockey star who said, "Don't skate to where the puck is. Skate to where it will be."

Release your dreams, imagine the world in which you want to live, and move toward it.

As you go through your day today, know all that you can, and embrace the fact there is much yet to know.

*Today's the day!*

# USING AND ABUSING POWER

UTILIZING POWER APPROPRIATELY IS AMONG THE MOST challenging human conditions to master. One of the great benefits that can be derived from power is not having to use it. My colleague General Colin Powell said, "Of all manifestations of power, restraint impresses people the most."

For more than 20 years, I have participated in an accountability group. We have a conference call every other Sunday night, and we answer a list of predetermined questions dealing with our personal and professional lives and the goals we are pursuing. One of the most poignant questions I answer every two weeks is, "Have you abused your power?" Power is a tool that can be used for good or bad. Ideally, power comes with a check and balance system that can keep it from spiraling out of control.

My late, great friend and colleague Brian Klemmer wrote an influential book titled *The Compassionate Samurai.* He hosted an international conference several times each year until his passing, and the conference continues as a significant part of his legacy. Brian's theory was that there are two kinds of people in the world: compassionate individuals who have great hearts, and powerful people he called samurai who have a lot of control and influence. He felt that when you can combine compassion and power, you can change the world for the better.

Twice each year, I continue to travel to a small island in Mission Bay near San Diego where both powerful and compassionate people from around the world gather to explore how to maximize their gifts. I have given over 40 speeches to this organization and believe my work with these unique people to be among the most fruitful of my career.

The appropriate utilizations of power generally involve a stimulus or trigger. The manifestation of power is best used as an effect and not a cause. President Teddy Roosevelt's admonition to "walk softly and carry a big stick" illustrates this well because if people know you have power but will only use it for good or to thwart evil, they come to respect but not fear your power.

I have visited the aircraft carrier named after President Roosevelt. The sailors who serve on that amazing vessel call it the "Big Stick." It is among the most powerful war machines ever known but can be an immense tool for peace and stability around the world. We all have power over others in our daily lives including friends, family, and coworkers. Power is best recognized and rarely used. Great power comes with great responsibility.

As you go through your day today, strive to use your power and never abuse it.

***Today's the day!***

# THE ULTIMATE LEGACY

THE BEGINNING OF A NEW YEAR OR ANY OTHER MILESTONE on the calendar gives us the opportunity to look back and to look forward.

As we peer into our past, it is best to focus on two areas: great memories we want to savor and important lessons we have learned from the life we have lived. Unfortunately, too often, we dwell on mistakes we have made and failures we have experienced and avoid the lesson we have learned. Those who do not learn from history are destined to repeat it.

As we look into our future, it is productive to set goals and objectives that we want to reach. If you take this process to its extreme, you will be planning your legacy. Planning how you wish to be remembered and what you want to leave behind is a great way to live your life.

The movie based on one of my novels was released on DVD—*The Ultimate Legacy* that stars Raquel Welch, Brian Dennehy, and Ali Hillis. It is the story of a wealthy and prominent woman, played by Raquel Welch, who discovers she has only one month to live. This creates a sense of urgency for her to establish her legacy. This exercise could benefit all of us whether we've got a month or a century to live.

My late, great friend and colleague Dr. Stephen Covey often said, "Begin with the end in mind." Following Dr. Covey's advice will cause you to live your life on purpose and with a mission.

I remember boarding a flight in Maui, Hawaii, that was headed back to the mainland. It was sunny, beautiful, and 82 degrees when we boarded the flight. Approximately eleven hours later, the plane landed in Chicago in the middle of a blizzard where it was 4 degrees below zero. I remember one elderly couple boarding the plane in Hawaii carrying their winter coats, scarves, and hats. While they were the object of some good-natured joking as the plane boarded in Maui, they were the objects of great envy and respect when the plane landed, and everyone faced blizzard conditions.

It is often hard to know what to do in the short term, but if you can spot a landmark or get a reliable compass reading, you can insure your journey will end well. Ancient sailors were often blown far from their original course, but if they could spot the North Star, they knew they could recalibrate their course and reach their destination.

If you can cherish your past victories while learning from your mistakes, as you plan your future which will culminate in your legacy, your priorities for today will become much more clear and easy to prioritize.

As you go through your day today, learn from your past, build your legacy, and enjoy it all.

*Today's the day!*

# About the Author

JIM STOVALL IS THE PRESIDENT OF NARRATIVE TELEVISION Network, as well as a published author of many books including *The Ultimate Gift*. He is also a columnist and motivational speaker. He may be reached at 5840 South Memorial Drive, Suite 312, Tulsa, OK 74145-9082; by email at Jim@JimStovall.com; on Twitter at www.twitter.com/stovallauthor; or on Facebook at www.facebook.com/jimstovallauthor.

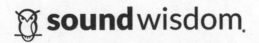